Introduction to Management

WITHDRAWN FROM
NESCOT

1 2 JAN 2022

A Guide for Better Business Performance

■

MALCOLM PEEL

the Institute
of Management

PITMAN PUBLISHING

The Institute of Management (IM) is at the forefront of management development and best management practice. The Institute embraces all levels of management from students to chief executives. It provides a unique portfolio of services for all managers, enabling them to develop skills and achieve management excellence. If you would like to hear more about the benefits of membership, please write to Department P, Institute of Management, Cottingham Road, Corby NN17 1TT. This series is commissioned by the Institute of Management Foundation.

W 658.4 PEE

Pitman Publishing
128 Long Acre, London WC2E 9AN

A Division of Longman Group UK Limited

First published in 1993

© Malcolm Peel 1993

A CIP catalogue record for this book can be obtained
from the British Library.

ISBN 0 273 03892 3

All rights reserved; no part of this publication may be reproduced, stored in a retrieval system, or transmitted in any form or by any means, electronic, mechanical, photocopying, recording, or otherwise without either the prior written permission of the Publishers or a licence permitting restricted copying issued by the Copyright Licensing Agency, 90 Tottenham Court Road, London W1P 9HE. This book may not be lent, resold, hired out or otherwise disposed of by way of trade in any form of binding or cover other than that in which it is published, without the prior consent of the Publishers.

Photoset in Linotron Century Schoolbook by
Northern Phototypesetting Co., Ltd., Bolton
Printed and bound by Bell and Bain Ltd., Glasgow

Contents

■

Acknowledgements

∎

In a subject as wide as this, specific acknowledgement is difficult; the content of this book clearly owes a debt, directly or indirectly, to so many sources. If they are not listed here, it is not for any lack of gratitude, but rather because of the difficulty of disentangling their many and varied contributions.

A number of leading authorities are mentioned in the text and to each of these I pay willing homage and give sincere thanks. In particular, I would like to mention my debt to Charles Kepner and Ben Tregoe. A number of passages in this book are based, as has been my own thinking for many years, on their teaching, especially on problem-solving and decision-making. I must also highlight the value to me of John Adair and his Action-Centred Leader approach, of the concept of the Managerial Grid developed by Blake and Mouton, and of Hersey and Blanchard's Situational Management, both mentioned in Chapter 12.

My most sincere thanks go to my colleague, Bob Norton, for his skilled preparation of the bibliography.

I would also like to express public and loving thanks to my ever-patient family, and most especially to my daughter Katherine for her thorough reading, methodical criticism, wise suggestions and, finally, her endless encouragement.

Malcolm Peel

Preface

■

Management is both an art and a science in its own right. To be effective managers require skills as distinct as those of any other profession. All too often, those who have succeeded in their chosen sphere find themselves promoted into a management post in which the skills they have used to achieve success are of no help; the fine classroom teacher, for example, who becomes a school head; the craftsman who is made into a foreman; the engineer promoted to engineering manager.

The aim of this book is to help those suffering, or who may suffer, in this way. It looks at management from a purely practical angle. Those who need a more academic approach are recommended to the books listed in the bibliography, although the present writer has to admit to seeing management as an area in which experienced pragmatism must reign supreme. The book is also designed to be read, rather than used purely for reference. For this reason also, those requiring more detailed treatment of specific subjects are invited to select from the bibliography.

Throughout, the reader is invited to relate the subject under discussion to his or her own experience through a number of checkpoints.

1

What is management?

- **What is management?**
- **The implications of the definition**
- **Other words with similar meanings**
- **The management sequence**
- **The resources of management**
- **The satisfactions and frustrations of managing**
- **The personal characteristics of managers**

L ike the art of poetry, life is not long enough, nor one book remotely sufficient, for the study of management. This chapter aims to clear the ground.

What is management

There are many definitions of management, some lengthy and scholarly. Originally, the word comes from the Latin 'manus', and refers to the driver controlling a team of horses pulling a cart or chariot by manipulating the reins. This image can be useful in considering other definitions.

The range of dictionary definitions of 'management' is quite surprising, but most of them can contribute something to our understanding of the underlying concept. Here are a few:

1. *To put a horse through its paces*

2. *To deal carefully – to husband (e.g. 'She managed the household budget with care')*

3. *To treat with indulgence*

4. *To be so unskilful or unlucky as to do something (e.g. 'He managed to knock over his glass of beer')*

5. *To continue to get along and pull through (e.g. 'He managed to get through the recession without being made redundant'.)*

Definitions by writers on management include:

6. *To forecast and plan, to organise, to command, to co-ordinate and to control* (Henri Fayol)

7. *Responsibility for so deciding the planning and regulating of the activities of people associated in a common task that the correct outcome is effectively and economically attained* (Brech)

8. *Working through individuals and groups to accomplish organisational goals* (Hersey and Blanchard)

9. *Personal command of a situation such that the technological, commercial and human aspects are interwoven into successful progress*

10. *The systematic organisation of economic resources* (Drucker)

11. *To be accountable to a higher authority for work which we do not carry out ourself*

12. *The decision-making element in a business.*

Despite the differences of emphasis, it is possible to pick out several key themes running through these: the need for goals or objectives for activity; the importance of the co-ordination of individual efforts and the fact that the direct work is largely or entirely done by someone other than the manager.

A simple preferred definition

Perhaps the simplest and most useful working definition of management is:

> **The achievement of objectives through other people**

This definition, like the others, is not perfect, but it can form a starting point for our thinking on the subject.

2

It suggests that the manager does not pull the chariot; he or she holds the reins and the whip to guide, motivate and control the team that does. Of course it is possible to push this analogy too far; managers who thought of their team as horses would not, today, get much work from them. But the picture is helpful in emphasising the key difference between managerial and other work. Non-managers perform tasks (at whatever level, from unskilled to highly professional) themselves.

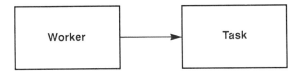

Managers, in so far as they are acting as managers, get others to do them:

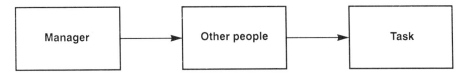

The implications of this definition

This definition of management has important practical implications:

- Management is a skill in its own right.
- Every job has some managerial elements, and no job is entirely managerial.
- Management is not necessarily a matter of seniority or salary.

Each of these is now considered.

Management is a skill in its own right

People frequently discuss whether it is possible to manage effectively work which they cannot perform themselves. Imagine, for example (assuming that you are not a time-served pattern-maker), that you are put in charge of a production shop of skilled pattern-makers. How likely is it that you could manage the shop effectively? What managerial disadvantages (if any) would you have over a time-served pattern-maker? What managerial advantages (if any) would you have over a time-served pattern-maker?

At some point in their careers, most managers will have to face the problem of managing people with skills they do not have, doing work they could not do. It is a situation that can worry the inexperienced manager, and even experienced managers can run into problems. It is discussed again in Chapter 7.

At the lower levels, especially as supervisors, experience of the work we must supervise can be a definite advantage. However, the more senior a manager becomes, the less important this will be. Managers cannot be confined to managing work they can carry out; at the higher levels, it is impossible for any one individual to be an expert in all the functions (e.g. finance, personnel, marketing) he or she may control.

Related to the ability to manage experts in unfamiliar fields is the skill of managing those who are older or more experienced than us. This too can be a daunting challenge for the young manager meeting it for the first time. Similar difficulties are often experienced by managers appointed from outside an organisation.

The concept of specific management competence, distinct from functional knowledge and skills, is fundamental. Knowledge is usually an advantage and management is no exception. Managers need to know where and how to get the knowledge they need, and will frequently employ other people to get it for them. The effective manager will have the other skills of management: the ability to question experts, understand their needs and problems, and give the support they need. They need to be masters more of the question than of the answer.

▶ **Checkpoint 1.1**

Have you ever managed people doing work you could not do yourself? If so, how did you get on, and what problems did you find? How did you set about overcoming your disadvantages in this situation? Did you feel you had any advantages over someone who had those skills? If you have never been in this situation, discuss it with someone who has.

Every job has some managerial content

Every worker must perform some tasks for themselves, and every worker must undertake some management. To do their job effectively, the tea boy or girl must ensure others provide the tea-bags, milk urn and trolley that they need to make and supply the tea. They must get others to let them have consumables as they are used, repair their equipment when it breaks down, and to supply new equipment when it is worn out. They must establish good relationships with their customers, so that they can complete their round smoothly and on time. These all involve achieving objectives through other people, and are management tasks. The consequences for their job of failure would be at least as serious as failure in the purely technical job of making the tea.

At the other end of the scale, even the most senior managers must carry out some work for themselves; total delegation is impractical and undesirable.

Management is not necessarily a matter of seniority

More senior jobs tend to have greater management content, although this is not always true. A senior professional (a company architect, for example, or a research engineer) may have little management responsibility, whilst a comparatively junior supervisor (say the foreman of a team of unskilled labourers) may have a job that is almost 100 per cent managerial in content.

5

▶ **Checkpoint 1.2**
Locate your own present and previous jobs on this graph. Has promotion increased the management content of your work? Has there been a clear progression in this way, or has the proportion of managerial work varied randomly from one job to the next?

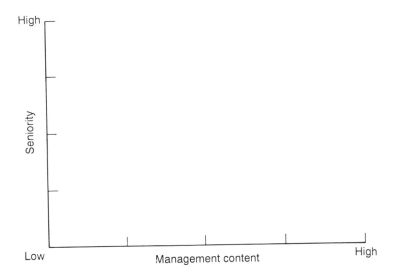

Many people say, when asked what career they would like to follow, 'I would like to be a manager'. However, the word is often used simply to mean 'getting to the top'. Some professionals, technologists and other specialists with little management responsibility are senior and better paid than many managers.

Many larger organisations now provide 'parallel promotion ladders' allowing specialists and professionals to progress without becoming managers. If this kind of opportunity does not exist, both the organisation and the individual will suffer. Many excellent classroom teachers, for example, have been forced to become mediocre school heads in order to get promotion; many brilliant engineers have become poor engineering managers.

▶ **Checkpoint 1.3**

Does your own organisation have a parallel promotion ladder? If so, what functions and up to what level does it apply? Given the choice, would you prefer to be a high level specialist/professional or a manager?

A variety of meanings

The word 'management' overlaps with several other common words including 'supervision', 'leadership', 'organisation', 'administration', 'control' and 'direction'. The word 'executive' is sometimes also used in this context, and 'boss' and 'governor' are in common use. It is helpful to consider the distinctions between them.

Supervision/supervisor

Supervisor is commonly used to indicate management at junior or first level, as carried out by chargehands, section leaders, foremen and supervisors. As such, it is identical to other kinds of management, and calls for the same skills. Indeed, many people at this level have a much greater management content in their work than many whose job title includes the word 'manager'.

Leadership/leader

The differences between a manager and a leader have practical importance. It can be approached by asking the twin questions:

6

1. Must managers be leaders?
2. Must leaders be managers?

The generally accepted answer to the first would be yes. If a manager's job is to achieve objectives through other people, it is inconceivable that he or she could be successful without leadership skills. Leadership is not the same as management, but it is an essential part of it.

On the other hand, to Question 2 most people would answer no. Successful leaders often rely on others to manage on their behalf. This is often the case with leaders of world-wide religious and political movements, and is equally true at lower levels. In practice, many charismatic leaders have no interest whatever in managing, and may be very bad at it. To manage an organisation or a movement led by such an individual can be a very challenging and stressful experience.

Execute/executive

Executive means a group or individual that 'executes' or carries out the decisions of another person or body. Thus the Civil Service is the executive body carrying out the wishes of Parliament, paid local government officials are the executive of their local council and managers in the private sector are the executives of their company's board.

However, the word 'executive' has been taken over, especially by those involved in selling, to convey simply the impression of high status; the 'executive model car', the 'executive suite' – even the 'executive briefcase'.

Organisation/organiser

Organisation is often used to mean an activity which has much in common with management, but may be inexactly defined:

'The committee asked Mary to organise the village fete.'

This statement leaves the degree of authority and responsibility that Mary was given unclear. It may, but probably does not, mean the same as:

'The committee asked Mary to manage the village fete.'

It is worth thinking about the distinctions between these statements and the practical implications they might have. Good organisation, of course, is an element in management, as in other work, and is discussed in Chapter 5.

Administration/administrator

Administration is sometimes used, especially in parts of the public sector, as synonymous with management:

> *'The hospital administrator represented the consultants at the meeting.'*

In more general use, 'administration' tends to have overtones of paperwork and systems, often without decision-making or the other elements of management:

> *'Administration of the competition has been fully computerised.'*

Direction/director

Directors holds posts within the private sector specified within company law; they are members of the board of a company, elected by share-holders to represent them. With that role come certain duties and res-ponsibilities.

Non-executive directors do not hold a paid position within the company; executive directors hold a paid position in addition to that of director. Executive directors thus have management as well as directorial res-ponsibilities, and in this role act as senior managers.

The title 'Director of . . . ' is sometimes used as an alternative to 'Head of . . . ' or 'Manager of . . . ' to indicate the most senior management post in a function, but without board membership.

Control/controller/comptroller

To control has, in general, a purely mechanical meaning:

> *'The operator controlled the feed of material into the hopper.'*

This is extended into one or two specialised areas, such as production control, or train control within a railway organisation. 'Controller' (or even the old-fashioned 'comptroller') is occasionally used as the title for senior managers within the financial function.

Boss

Boss is probably the most common word for manager. Its origin provides one view of the manager's job. A boss is the central stone or piece of wood

8

in an arch or dome, towards which the ribs converge and against which they lean. Without the boss, the whole structure would collapse.

Governor

Governor is derived from the Latin word, 'gubernator', meaning the steersman of a ship; the individual who sets the course and ensures that the ship follows it.

▶ **Checkpoint 1.4**

Do the job titles in your organisation reflect the real nature of the jobs? If not, how could they be improved?

The management sequence

9

Every complete act of management has four phases:
- Planning
- Organising
- Implementing
- Controlling

Logically, the four follow each other in what may be called the 'management sequence', and the results from following the sequence may be used to initiate a further set of actions. See Figure 1.1.

Because they are in many cases working through other people, work in each of these phases may actually be done by someone else, but it will the manager's responsibility to ensure they are completed to their satisfaction.

Fig. 1.1 The basic management sequence

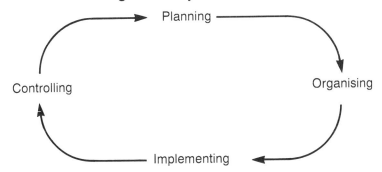

On many day-to-day occasions, all the phases may only take a few moments' thought at most. Quite naturally, the manager will ask himself questions such as:

Planning questions
> *'What am I driving at here?'*
> *'What outcome do I want from this?'*

Organising questions
> *'How can I get people and equipment where they're needed?'*
> *'Who will do what, and when?'*

Implementation questions
> *'Has Bill started work yet?'*
> *'Did that stuff come from the printers this morning?*

Control questions
> *'How do we compare with budget?'*
> *'How can I find a replacement for those faulty parts?'*

Within each phase of the sequence, the manager will have three essential tasks:

- Problem-solving
- Decision-making
- Communication

In carrying out these, the manager will ask questions such as:

Problem-solving questions
> *'What, precisely, has gone wrong here?'*
> *'When, exactly, did the fault start?'*
> *'What similar or related things have **not** gone wrong?'*
> *'What are the differences between the two?'*

Decision-making questions
> *'What has already been agreed, and what remains to be agreed?'*
> *'What alternative courses of action are open to us?'*
> *'Which is the best choice in the present circumstances?'*

Communication questions
> *'Who needs to know about this, and what do they need to know?'*
> *'How can I best get this message across?'*

The complete process can thus be represented as shown in Figure 1.2.

Fig. 1.2 The process of management

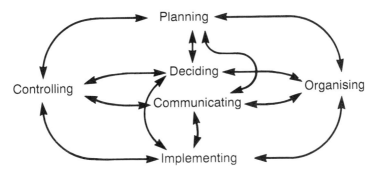

▶ **Checkpoint 1.5**

Consider the last important task you have undertaken at work. Did you go through all the elements of the Management Sequence? If not, did you have valid reasons for not completing them all, or would it have been better if you had?

The resources of management

To achieve anything, managers must make good use of the resources at their disposal. These resources will be both a source of strength and a constraint. Often, they will be alternative to each other – if we had more time, we would not need so much cash; if we had a machine, we would not need the skilled staff, and so on.

The most important resources include:

- People/skills/knowledge
- Machinery and equipment
- Materials
- The market
- Time
- Finance
- Products and processes
- Information
- Buildings/sites/land
- Infrastructure/location
- Goodwill/reputation/image

Most of these are the subject, in larger organisations, of a specialist function. Thus a Personnel or Human Resources function will have responsibility for aspects of the people resource; a Marketing function for aspects of the market; a Finance or Accounting function for finance; a Public Relations or Public Affairs for reputation and image, and so on. Some, such as information, are organised in a wide range of differing ways. But every manager has the responsibility for striving to get the resources he or she needs, and then using them to best advantage. Resources are for them to use, not the specialists. The Personnel Manager, for example, does not control the people resource – but is available to help, advise and support other managers in doing so. The Computer Manager should not control the computing resource, but support other managers in their use of it.

The role of functions within an organisation is discussed in more detail in Chapter 5.

▶ **Checkpoint 1.6**

Are you short of any of the resources you need to do your job effectively? If so, which and why?

The satisfactions and frustrations of management

As with most occupations, management has its own characteristic satisfactions and, sadly, it also has its own characteristic frustrations.

THE SATISFACTIONS OF MANAGEMENT

■ Producing a profit or contribution

■ Working through people

■ Producing identifiable changes in the real world

■ Solving tough, practical problems

■ Overcoming obstacles

■ Making decisions

■ Working in a demanding, continually changing environment

THE FRUSTRATIONS OF MANAGEMENT

- Overload and continuing stress
- Inability to overcome irrational or uncontrollable difficulties
- Chronic personality clashes
- Conflicting and changing priorities
- Working in a demanding, continually changing environment

▶ **Checkpoint 1.7**
What job satisfactions and frustrations do you feel most strongly in your present post?

13

The personal characteristics of managers

There is no typical manager. There are as many different ways of achieving management success as there are personalities: 'There's more than one way to skin a cat'. However, there are a few traits of character which may make it easier for an individual to manage.

CHARACTERISTICS THAT MAY HELP INDIVIDUALS TO MANAGE

- Tough-mindedness
- Extroversion
- The ability to tolerate ambiguity and uncertainty
- Enjoyment of power
- Decisiveness
- Persistence
- The ability to think on one's feet
- The butterfly mind
- Intuitive understanding of others
- High tolerance of stress

As has already been stressed, there is no one profile of the perfect manager. However, there are also some character traits which may make it harder for an individual to manage successfully and with enjoyment.

CHARACTERISTICS THAT MAY MAKE IT HARDER FOR INDIVIDUALS TO MANAGE

- Self-consciousness and shyness
- Perfectionism, especially in details
- A strongly rational approach
- A desire to pursue knowledge for its own sake
- The desire to allocate family or out-of-work activities a high priority
- A kind and gentle nature

▶ **Checkpoint 1.8**

Which of your characteristics do you feel are of most help to you in managing effectively? Which, if any, hold back your effectiveness as a manager?

2

Leadership

- ■ **Motivation**
- ■ **Objective setting**
- ■ **Setting an example**
- ■ **Personal relationships**
- ■ **Delegation**
- ■ **Team leadership**

Whilst, as was suggested in the last chapter, many leaders are not managers, to succeed the manager must be an effective leader. The description 'a born leader' is common, and there can be no doubt that leading comes more naturally to some than to others. However, as with all skills, there is much that everyone can do to improve their effectiveness. This chapter suggests some of the key points.

Ensuring that things actually happen and objectives are met despite difficulties and resistance is the essence of management. As managers, we will not always succeed, but excuses for failure become us less well than other people. In our own area, the buck stops with us.

▶ **Checkpoint 2.1**
Who is the best leader you have worked with in any (work or non-work) field? What made them such an effective leader? Were they also an effective manager? What are your weaknesses and strengths as a leader?

Motivation

To lead people, we must motivate them. Many of the finest leaders have an instinctive understanding of what motivates others. But even if we have this, it is helpful to become familiar with the work of the leading authorities in this crucial area.

The study of motivation at work has for long been associated with a small number of well-known names. These include: Elton Mayo (the 'Hawthorne Experiment'); Douglas McGregor ('Theory X and Theory Y'); A H Maslow ('The hierarchy of needs'); and F W Hertzberg ('hygiene factors'). Each of these has made a major contribution to management theory, and in doing so, each has helped practical managers at every level. Those who are not familiar with their work will find it interesting and helpful; details are included in the bibliography.

COMPARING OTHERS' MOTIVATION WITH OUR OWN

If two groups of managers are asked to say what motivates them and what they believe motivates those who work for them, there are often striking differences in the replies. The group considering the motivation of those who work for them tend to place money at the top of the list, with job security a close second. On the other hand, the group considering their own motivation claim to be motivated by factors such as the desire to do a job well, to contribute to the success of their organisation, to be recognised and respected by their colleagues and to better society as a whole.

The exercise can be conducted at any level in an organisation with the same results. It seems to demonstrate that people tend to ascribe higher-level motivation to themselves than they do to those who work for them, whom they tend to regard as simple, selfish souls motivated only by filthy lucre. Managers who do think in this way will not get the best out of others.

INDIVIDUAL MOTIVATION

Motivation is in any case a more individual matter than we sometimes think. It is the mainspring of personality, and the mix of factors is different for each of us. It will change over time; few of us are motivated in the same way at the age of 50 as we were at 20. It will vary according to circumstances; our motivation during a boring meeting will not be the same as when enjoying an intimate meal for two. Our motivation will be strongly influenced by any group of which we feel part, whether a football crowd, a regiment or a revivalist meeting.

Managers who wish to motivate their people need to understand the distinctive sources of their motivation. One may place care for a sick child at the top of their list; another, time spent in a favourite sport. One person's actions may spring from a powerful urge to prove themselves to their parents, or do better than a brother or sister; another from deep religious conviction. For some, love of animals is paramount; for others, a desire to see their organisation grow and prosper beyond its rivals. The list is endless, and the combinations infinite.

Some factors operate positively, disposing us towards a belief or a course of action; some operate negatively, steering us away. The balance between positive and negative will change, sometimes suddenly, as when an opinion is expressed in a discussion by someone we hate. Negative factors – hate, jealousy, fear – are sometimes stronger than the positive, but here too generalisation is dangerous.

We must beware of over-simplifying, or of attributing our motivation to others. There is no substitute for knowledge of individuals.

17

DO'S AND DON'TS: MOTIVATION

Here are some guidelines for practical motivation:

DO'S AND DON'TS OF MOTIVATION	
Do	**Don't**
■ Agree clear goals	
■ Ask for suggestions	■ Be possessive of ideas
■ Give genuine praise	■ Sound dogmatic
■ Express genuine appreciation	■ Creep
■ Register agreement	■ Make unfavourable comparisons
■ Be enthusiastic but not gushing	■ Try to win the argument
■ Set a good example	■ Say 'Do as I say, not as I do.'
■ Look to future success	■ Look at past failure

▶ **Checkpoint 2.2**

List your own personal long-term motivators. Consider both positive and negative factors. Do the same for one or more people who work with you. How effective is your boss at motivating you and others? What can you learn from him or her about motivation?

Objective setting

Objective setting is one of the most powerful tools of management and an essential element of leadership. To lead effectively, we must be clear what objectives we wish to attain, and make them clear to those we are leading. It is not enough to have a general desire to advance; we must decide which hilltop we intend to capture, and the route we will follow to get there.

GOOD OBJECTIVES

To be effective, objectives must meet the 'Five-C' criteria:

- Clearly stated
- Consistent with other objectives
- Checkable – preferably measurable
- Challenging
- Carry-outable (achievable)

SHORT AND LONG-TERM OBJECTIVES

Objectives may be long-term; associated with a particular project:

> *To reduce the proportion of rejects to less than one per cent.*

> *To ensure the new plant is commissioned by 1st January 1994.*

> *To introduce flexible working without a strike.*

But objectives can be of great value in the short term also:

> *To empty the in-tray before close of work today.*

> *To learn the new fire regulations by heart before coffee break.*

> *To produce the minutes of the meeting before the MD leaves.*

THE USES OF OBJECTIVES

Objectives are part of many management processes. The use of objectives for decision-making is discussed in Chapter 9, and the setting of performance objectives is referred to in Chapter 6.

Objectives have been used by some organisations as a comprehensive system of management, originally developed by Drucker – *Management by objectives (MBO)*. Used in this way, objectives are set for the whole organisation and for the departments and individuals within it, at regular intervals. Performance is reviewed against these objectives. The concept of MBO has been of great help, but in practice the procedures may tend to become bureaucratic and time-consuming. It is now rarely used as a complete system.

▶ **Checkpoint 2.3**
Have you got clear long-term objectives? If so, were you involved in setting them? Do they help?

Setting an example

'Do as I say, not as I do' is a message that quickens few pulses. Whilst being a paragon of virtue is not, luckily for most of us, a prerequisite of management, setting a good example is. There are a number of key areas.

Leaders must be:

■ Committed
■ Honest
■ Self-disciplined
■ Courageous
■ Loyal

COMMITMENT

'I couldn't care less' is not the slogan of a leader. To gain the commitment of others, managers must be committed themselves. Those who show that they do not care about the achievement of the organisation's objectives, or the maintenance of its standards, cannot expect that others will care. Nothing destroys morale more effectively than for a manager to indicate that he or she does not care for what the organisation is aiming to do. Such an attitude is difficult to hide; the manager's true attitude is quickly apparent to those who work in his or her area.

This does not mean that managers must agree with everything they are asked to do, or life would be impossible. Any intelligent and independent-minded manager may find reasons for disagreeing with policy and methods, or may experience difficulty in getting on with some of their own bosses. But there is a clear difference between this kind of disagreement (which, in fact, often arises from a deep commitment) and lack of commitment to the organisation as a whole.

▶ **Checkpoint 2.4**

Have you ever worked for a boss who did not appear committed to the organisation? What were the effects of this? What was the eventual outcome? How deep is your own commitment to your organisation? If you have any problems in this area, how do you feel they can be resolved?

HONESTY

Every manager lives in a glasshouse. With the eyes of everyone who works for him or her forever on them, the dishonest manager has serious problems. Managers must be pure in areas in which others may be prepared to bend the rules. We must beware of fiddling expenses. We must beware of purloining our employer's property, even in small things. We cannot contemplate manipulating time sheets or clock cards. Even white lies, such as whether we are in or available, can come back to haunt us.

Problems with minor dishonesties can sometimes arise when a manager is promoted within his or her own area. The little fiddles and bendings of the rules that he or she may have shared, suddenly become something to be condemned. Those awaiting promotion in their own area please note!

▶ **Checkpoint 2.5**

Have you experienced problems with honesty at work in any form? If so, what were the consequences?

SELF-DISCIPLINE

Managers must, to motivate their people, demonstrate a high level of self-discipline. If our time-keeping is poor, we cannot expect our people's time-keeping to be good. If we take long lunches, disappear into town in the middle of the morning, or regularly sneak off early on Friday afternoons, we will soon find others doing the same.

Discipline must also apply to working practices. We must not smoke where smoking is not allowed, we must wear safety glasses and hard hats where required, operate machinery correctly, and follow procedures.

Lack of self-discipline in more personal matters can also destroy our effectiveness. Scruffy dress or turnout will raise questions. The manager who drinks during the working day will have problems. Managers involved in a questionable relationship with a colleague or member of their own staff may destroy their standing.

21

▶ **Checkpoint 2.6**
Have you ever been affected by a manager's lack of self discipline? If so, what and how? Are you well-disciplined in all important respects at work?

COURAGE

Leadership is best done from the front. Because they are leaders, managers cannot afford to show fear in a working context. Jobs involving physical dangers – leading in the armed forces, the police, fire or rescue services, for example – obviously call for physical courage in the leader. In the more common situations of commercial and industrial management, moral courage is indispensable. Reluctance to make a critical decision, face an angry customer, or sort out an undisciplined subordinate will be spotted, and harm the manager's credibility. Those who face such situations with courage will gain in status as a leader.

▶ **Checkpoint 2.7**
Have you experienced fear in a working situation? How did you cope?

LOYALTY

Loyalty breeds loyalty. Managers must be loyal in every direction; to their boss, to their colleagues and to their subordinates. If we are not loyal to our own boss, we will have difficulty in commanding loyalty from those who work for us. Loyalty to colleagues can be the biggest test of all, but our role as a leader will be much harder in its absence.

As with commitment to the organisation as a whole, the need for loyalty does not imply unquestioning acceptance of everything that is thrown at us. But everyone recognises the difference between honest and open disagreement and sniping, festering, disloyalty.

▶ **Checkpoint 2.8**

Have you ever worked for a boss who was disloyal to his boss or others within the organisation? If so, what was the effect? Do you find problems with your own loyalty in any direction? If so, how? How can the situation be improved?

Personal relationships

As managers, it is difficult to lead people with whom we do not have a sound personal relationship.

HOW CLOSE?

The closeness of our relationships will vary. We will naturally know those with whom we work on a daily basis well. If we have a large or widely-scattered team, it may be difficult to know everyone to the same extent. Good managers will make a special effort to get to know those they do not meet so often.

Small points make a big difference. Managers who do not know their people's names will cause offence; those who mix them up (however big their empire) will cause deep resentment. On the other hand, if we can remember names, faces, jobs and one or two salient personal facts (where they are going on holiday, the team they support, when their child sits GCSEs) we will start several points up.

A few subordinates prefer to remain private and uninvolved, keeping their personal and working lives separate. In situations in which the closest teamwork and the most demanding environment are involved (a polar expedition, for example, or active military service) this may create problems. In ordinary situations it does not. We must not try to force a degree of unwanted intimacy on our people.

Relationships must be two-way. Most people want to feel they know their boss as a person. New and insecure managers often keep too great a distance between themselves and their people; this can cause problems. If we give nothing of ourself to those who work with us, they will see us as stand-offish, possibly snobbish. It is likely that, to fill in the gaps in their knowledge of us, they may even invent a character and biography. If they do, it is certain not to be flattering.

In civilian organisations today, the need to maintain an artificial gap between managers and managed ('officers and their ladies, NCOs and their wives, other ranks and their women . . .') has almost disappeared. A few still have, for example, separate eating facilities – the directors' dining room, staff restaurant and works canteen – although this is now less common. Organisations with a Japanese culture expect employees of every level to wear the same uniform.

Some managers find it difficult to manage those they have previously known as friends and equals. A relationship that is too close can give an appearance of favouritism. Those who manage people of the opposite sex always risk the misunderstanding which a close relationship can cause.

▶ **Checkpoint 2.9**
How close is your relationship with your boss? Would it be better if it was closer or less close?

FAIRNESS

As managers, we forfeit the right to laugh at the clumsy or ridicule the unpopular. Whilst it is impossible to eliminate personal feelings, they must affect our work as little as possible. We must give equal treatment to all: praise, blame, rough jobs and opportunities must be shared out even-handedly.

Like other relationships, that between manager and managed depends on personal integrity. And just as some spouses cheat on their partners, so managers can cheat on their subordinates. There are many ways of cheating.

> ## CHEATING ON YOUR SUBORDINATES
> - Take credit for their achievements
> - Blame your failings on the subordinate
> - Fail to share reward and praise fairly
> - Criticise them behind their back
> - Block opportunities for promotion
> - Withhold information or deliberately mislead them

Such behaviour strikes at the root of effective leadership.

▶ Checkpoint 2.10

Has a boss of yours ever seriously cheated you. If so, how? Have you ever deliberately cheated one of your subordinates?

SUPPORT

A manager who bends with every wind, or, worst of all, is prepared to stab us in the back will have few followers. If we want people to follow our leadership, they must feel that they can rely on our support.

No-one is free from criticism, and our operation will be no exception. Sooner or later, our internal or external customers will find fault with someone in our team. The way we tackle the situation will be crucial. We must support our people in public to the utmost of our power, whatever investigation or reprimand may later take place behind closed doors.

As managers, we are 'problem-solvers of last resort'; the buck stops with us. Ultimately, ours is the task of ensuring that the machinery, equipment, materials and consumables our people need are duly provided. We are responsible for seeing they are paid, and that they receive the organisational facilities due to them.

In providing support we must avoid always taking others' problems on to our shoulders. It is often better to help people to solve their own problems. We can listen actively, ask perceptive questions, challenge their preconceptions, offer clues and suggest sources of help or courses of action. By doing this, we will develop them and help them tackle similar problems in the future. Once in a while we may decide that intervention would make matters worse. Occasionally and for valid reasons, not noticing a problem can become a very delicate art.

The word 'empowerment' has recently come into fashion. As with most buzz-words, its meaning varies according to who is using it, but the basic idea is that management should be less directive and more enabling. Those managed should be 'empowered' by their manager, thus releasing their innate skills for use on the task in hand. Another word sometimes used to express this approach is that the manager should be a 'facilitator', who removes obstacles and smooths the path for his or her people.

▶ **Checkpoint 2.11**
Has a manager ever failed to support you in an important matter, or reprimanded you publicly? How did you feel about it? Have you ever made the same mistake?

Delegation

25

Delegation is essential to effective leadership. Not only is it the best way of coping with a large amount of work; it is one of the soundest methods of developing people. But newly-appointed managers frequently find delegation difficult. It is always easy to find excuses for not delegating.

EXCUSES FOR NOT DELEGATING

- *'I would do it better myself.'*
- *'It would take longer for me to explain than for them to do.'*
- *'Delegation is running away from the problem.'*
- *'They would think I was exploiting them.'*
- *'I want the brownie points all to myself.'*

We must overcome such feelings, and accept that, done properly at the proper time, delegation is essential to good management.

WHEN TO DELEGATE

- When it provides a good opportunity to develop and train someone
- When one of our people has a higher level of skill than we do
- When it would offer an opportunity for one of our people to shine
- When we have insufficient time, and someone else has enough
- When we wish to motivate and show our confidence in someone

Delegation should be a frequent occurrence. The way delegation is carried out is all-important. Good briefing is essential.

HOW TO DELEGATE

We must explain:

- Why we have decided to delegate (If there is anything unusual about the circumstances)
- Why we have chosen them (If others might have been chosen)
- What the objectives of the task are and how their success will be measured
- What constraints (such as time or finance) will apply
- What resources (other than those normally available) may be used for the task
- That we will be available to advise, but otherwise leave the task confidently in their hands

After we have briefed the person, we must sit back and leave the individual to get on without breathing over their shoulder.

► **Checkpoint 2.12**

Do you frequently delegate work? If not, why not? Is your own boss good at delegating? Can you learn from him or her, either what to do or not to do?

Team leadership

Many managers claim, airily, to lead 'teams', but the fact that people work together – even on the same tasks or in the same office – does not

26

make them a team. Teams do not just happen. Building and leading a real team requires much hard, careful work, as many football managers know to their cost. It involves far more than leading each individual in it.

The additional ingredients include:

- Involving the team in setting its mission and objectives
- Ensuring clear definition of roles
- Knowing and taking account of individual strengths
- Holding regular team meetings
- Undertaking joint development activities
- Ensuring an efficient flow of communication throughout the team
- Being sensitive to interpersonal problems
- Conducting joint assessments of progress against objectives, and joint solving of problems

THE TEAM MISSION AND OBJECTIVES

27

Possibly even more than individuals, teams need to know what their goals are, and how they can be scored. Joint setting of objectives and discussion of strategy is essential.

DEFINITION OF ROLES

Inspiring a group of brilliant and not-so-brilliant individuals to play together and in the same direction can be hard work. Members need to know what position they are expected to play, and to feel confident that it really belongs to them. We must recognise their skills and interests, and not insist on our most accomplished forward playing in goal. If members know and respect each other's skills, they are more likely to pass them the ball. In the rough and tumble of the game, they will be happier standing in for an injured colleague, or undertaking an unexpected role, if they have the secure knowledge that it will not affect their regular position.

Meredith Belbin[1] has defined eight typical roles, within which he believes most people tend to act in a group situation. However, it is possible to apply this concept too rigidly; in practice, individuals will adopt different roles in different groups, and will show a range of behaviour even within the same group.

[1] *Management Teams – Why they Succeed or Fail*, Heinemann, 1981.

REGULAR TEAM MEETINGS

Teams that never meet will never gel. Good meetings, at which progress is jointly reviewed and problems jointly solved, can be the essence of team working. However, if meetings are too frequent or badly conducted, they can be counter-productive. Running effective meetings is discussed in Chapter 8.

JOINT DEVELOPMENT ACTIVITIES

To build a team without training together should be unthinkable, but many managers try it. Training as a team kills two birds with one stone; we improve individual skills whilst building the team spirit. If, as the team leader, we take a full part, this will increase the value of the training greatly.

28

Such joint development may not necessarily be directly work-related; weekend outdoor or adventure training can be very powerful. 'Sensitivity training' such as 'T-groups', designed to increase members' awareness of group dynamics and the effect of their behaviour on others has been found helpful in some circumstances.

There are dangers in team training if the team is not functioning well. If there are personal tensions, exposing individuals to criticism or showing their weakness may make matters worse. The leader must also be secure and mature enough to expose any weaknesses and not to seek to dominate.

▶ **Checkpoint 2.13**
Have you been involved in any team development activities? How helpful did you find them, and how could you have improved them?

THE EFFICIENT FLOW OF COMMUNICATION

Team members need to be kept in touch: to know what is going on and what their colleagues are up to. If they are scattered geographically (even in different rooms or parts of a building) we must, as the leader, make sure that communications flow.

SENSITIVITY TO INTERPERSONAL PROBLEMS

The dynamics of a team can help or hinder its leader. Group dynamics – the way relationships between the members develop and function – are complex and can sometimes be surprising.

High amongst the problems may be the emergence of an unofficial leader who commands more respect than the manager. This may happen for many reasons, including the personality of the two individuals; their pre-existing relationships with the other members of the group (one, for example, may have been a member for some time – the other may be a newcomer); or their relative competence in areas of work. A trade union position, such as convenor or shop steward, may produce the same effect.

There are many other ways in which relationships between team members may make the manager's role harder. Friendships may be too close, causing loss of time from gossip and chatter. There may be friction which prevents colleagues from working properly together. Occasionally one member of the group may become totally isolated from the rest, who refuse to have any contact. The web of relationships within a mature team can be very complex and so close that a new manager is excluded.

Facing problems such as these demands a high degree of sensitivity on the part of the manager. We must understand what goes on in the team before attempting an intervention or risk making matters worse. At the end of the day, managers must lead, and find the appropriate way of building and maintaining the necessary authority.

▶ **Checkpoint 2.14**
Are you aware of any problems in the dynamics of your team? How do you feel they could be solved?

JOINT PROGRESS ASSESSMENT AND JOINT PROBLEM SOLVING

As with individuals, so with teams; they need to feel valued, and wish to develop. Joint reviews of their achievements are essential; this is not the same as being told what they have achieved (or failed to achieve) by their manager. Joint problem-solving also builds teams in a way that an imposed solution never could. Few things are more powerful in developing a team than the knowledge that it has, as a team, overcome obstacles.

The role of managers will be to set the situations up; calling the team together, outlining the situation, providing a framework, and acting as facilitator. This is true 'empowerment' at work; the manager who can do this will unleash an immense fund of knowledge, skill and commitment.

► **Checkpoint 2.15**

Does your team engage in joint problem-solving and progress reviews? If so, how helpful are they? If not, do you feel they would be of value?

3

Self management

> - **Self organisation**
> - **Priority setting**
> - **Time management**
> - **Stress and health management**
> - **Self development**

The manager who cannot manage him or herself will have difficulty in managing others.

Self organisation

Organisation is an essential part of the Management Sequence (Chapter 1). Some managers find it easier to organise others than themselves. They enjoy the big canvas, and are switched on by the important assignment. Details bore them. They are switched off by what they see as the trivia of their working life; their papers, their notes, their desks, their diaries. Managers must certainly, as Peters[1] says 'thrive on chaos'; they must be able to tolerate rough edges, imprecision and ambiguity. But for some, the worst chaos is in their own office.

To be unable to find the piece of paper we desperately need, to miss the train or to forget the crucial meeting can undo weeks of effective management. It will waste our time and that of others, fray tempers and damage relationships, set a bad example, and may easily lead to mistaken decisions.

It is for this reason that managers have traditionally found immense help in the support of a good secretary. But the establishment of typing

[1] Tom Peters, *Thriving on Chaos: a Handbook for Management Revolution*, Macmillan, 1988.

pools, audio typing, the growth of personal computing and general economies have made this less readily available. Many managers who do still have at least a shared secretary, do not make proper use of them. Manager and secretary should form a close team, within which there is trust and openness. A good manager will delegate much to a good secretary, and never let pride or status stand in the way of learning from and using to the full the secretary's skill and knowledge.

Whether or not we have secretaries, self-management cannot be delegated. It is an attitude to ourself and our work that must form the base from which we manage others.

▶ **Checkpoint 3.1**

How tidy is your desk? When were you last late for an appointment? Do you have a secretary? If so, what use do you make of your secretary? Are there ways in which he or she could be of more help to you?

32

Priority setting

There are few more frustrating things than to work for a manager who continually changes his or her priorities. At best, such behaviour is annoying – at worst, destructive. But setting and keeping priorities is never easy.

The more easily people can get to us, the greater the risk. There is always a balance to be struck between 'open door management' and allowing those who work for us so much freedom that they disturb our priorities.

In theory, setting priorities does not make for less work. In practice, it is an immense help. If our priorities are correct, we will not to waste time on unimportant business, and many concerns will have solved themselves before we get around to them.

Many managers start the day by listing the tasks they have to do. Sometimes, producing the list is sufficient – the priorities are clear on first inspection.

On other occasions, we may need to take rather more time to set a rational order. To do this, we should consider each aspect separately:

- Importance
- Urgency
- Time to completion

The *importance* of a concern can be judged by the answer to the question 'What would happen if I took no action about this?' The *urgency* can be judged by the answer to 'What is the effect of delaying action on this?' The *time to completion* is the answer to 'How long will it take me to deal with this?'

It can be difficult to distinguish between importance and urgency, but the difference matters. Three examples may help:

Urgent but not important:
Tidying my desk before the chief executive arrives in three minutes.

Important but not urgent:
Finding a new product to replace one that has done so well for the past five years.

Important and urgent:
Repairing the fault that brought the production line to a standstill.

Urgent concerns will usually be dealt with first in order of importance, followed by concerns that can be dealt with very quickly, even if unimportant, and finally the longer tasks, again in order of importance.

With a long and difficult list, we may need to spend time making a thorough assessment. It can help to rank the list against each aspect. The priority will then be the reverse order of the total of the rankings:

	Importance	Urgency	Time to Completion	Total	Priority
Tidying my desk	3	1=	1	5	2
Finding a new product	1=	3	3	7	3
Repairing the line	1=	1=	2	4	1

Sadly, having neatly arranged our priorities, a new concern usually comes along which may disturb them. We will continually need to check that our order of priorities is still valid. However, if we have established our priorities rationally, we will have an instrument to assess where any newcomers should be placed on the list, and whether changed circumstances have changed the order.

► **Checkpoint 3.2**

Do you have problems in setting and keeping priorities? If so, why? Is there action you can take to make it easier, either by rational setting and checking, or by identifying the cause of the problem and eliminating it?

Time management

As a resource, time is unique. If we lose a pound, we may find it, or earn another; if a valued colleague leaves for a better job, we can seek a replacement: but if we lose a minute, it can never be replaced.

Some managers always seem to need more time. They are for ever doing six things as once. A queue of visitors crowds their office whilst both telephones are ringing and their secretary stands with an urgent note from the MD. They are always too busy to listen properly. They arrive early and stay late, but still take home bulging briefcases every night. They go in at weekends, and take little or none of their annual leave. Their personal life suffers; if asked what they do in their spare time, they reply: 'What spare time?'

Other managers doing the same job seem to find more hours in the day and more days in the week. They always have time to listen and talk with their people. They rarely work late or take work home. If problems arise, they have time to cope with them. They keep methodical diaries, and know where they must be and when. They have an enviable leisure life and wonderful holidays.

A few managers really enjoy the feeling of being overloaded. It switches them on, and brings out their best. If they were not, they would feel unwanted and unappreciated. Sometimes the culture of the organisation is such that managers who do not appear rushed off their feet are branded as passengers. In most organisations it takes considerable courage for managers to sit still, however hard they may be thinking. But most of us detest the feeling of overload, and would like to manage our time better. To achieve this, the following steps will help:

- Find out how your time is spent
- Plan time use methodically
- Avoid the time-stealers
- Streamline
- Use marginal time

FINDING OUT HOW OUR TIME IS SPENT

The starting point for improving time management is to establish how we spend it now. We can keep a full time-use diary, or sample our activities methodically. Either will use time in itself, but to do so for a short period – perhaps a month – can pay big dividends afterwards.

The time-use diary

The time-use diary should be very simple; two columns on ruled pages are sufficient. The first column will be used to record the time when every change of activity occurs; the second to record what the new activity is. A page might look like the example in the box:

TIME MANAGEMENT DIARY	
Time	Activity
0835	Drive to work
0855	Check diary for day
0859	Bob enters; talks about holiday
0910	Phone; Jane sick, not coming in
0914	Bob leaves; visit Personnel to fix substitute for Jane

The diary should give sufficient detail to remind us later what was going on. It is essential that it tells what *actually* happened, not what *should* have happened! If we are gossiping or searching for a lost file, we must say so, if the diary is to be of any value.

Activity sampling

It may be less time-consuming in itself to sample what we are doing at regular intervals. The interval we choose must not be so short that we spend our whole time sampling, not so long that we miss many activities. Usually intervals of 10 or 15 minutes are suitable. At the start of each, we note down what we are doing. The sampling must continue for a sufficient period. Depending on how routine our job is, from one to four weeks is usually adequate. As with the diary, we must record enough detail to be meaningful later, and if we are not honest, the point of the exercise will be lost.

Whichever method has been used we can, at the end of the period of observation, total the entries for each type of activity, and calculate each as a percentage of the overall total. We can thus produce a ranked list of the proportions of our time spent in each activity. A simple classification would include receiving telephone calls, making calls, meetings, one-to-one discussions, writing, reading, walking round the building or the site, travelling, searching for papers and filling in spare minutes. We may decide to include a breakdown by the various assignments we are working on, or perhaps the clients we work for.

This will give us a clear picture of how our time is being used. There are often big surprises, and simply to complete the exercise may be enough to show how we can save many hours a week.

▶ **Checkpoint 3.3**

Do you really know how your working time is spent, and how much of it is productive? If not, why not find out?

36

PLAN TIME USE METHODICALLY

There are three common tools for time planning:

- The simple list
- The appointment diary
- The organiser

For many, the most effective form of short-term time planning is to produce, at the start of each day, a list of tasks to be completed. Some people prefer to set objectives to be achieved rather than tasks; this can give a stronger sense of purpose, and may allow more flexibility of approach. Either can be combined with priority setting in the way described above, and produces a sound basis for the day's work.

Longer-term time planning calls for an appointment diary. Simple as this sounds, some managers have perpetual problems with methodical diary keeping. We probably have more than one diary; on our desk, in our pocket, on our secretary's desk and the kitchen wall at home. The fewer diaries we keep, the less the scope for error: keeping all up to date is demanding but essential.

It also helps to establish rules about which is our master diary, and who is allowed to make entries in it. If we have a secretary, they should be clear whether they can commit us to an appointment. Some managers leave their desk diary open in their absence, and invite others to check them and write in appointments; this can save much to-and-froing.

Some people find 'organisers' a help in planning time. Several well-known designs are available, some supported by training courses. Others have found that they lack the discipline or interest to keep organisers up-to-date after the first few days. Electronic organisers are fun to play with, but they too demand effort if they are to give real help. Neither is a short cut.

▶ **Checkpoint 3.4**
Are you good at diary-keeping? How many diaries do you have? Who do you allow to make appointments for you? Have you used an organiser of any kind, and if so, did you keep it up-to-date?

AVOIDING THE TIME STEALERS

Napoleon said that he never bothered to answer letters, because he found that eventually they all answered themselves. We are not Napoleon, but his motto may help in dealing with 'junk' mail. Certainly the first question to be asked, not only about answering letters, but about any other activity, is: 'Is this necessary?'. The next question should be: 'If so, why?'

Routine activities can be the worst time stealers. Regular meetings – every day, week, or month – are amongst the worst offenders. It is always possible to fill the agenda; but is there really an adequate justification for the time taken? If the meeting is necessary, do we need to be there? If we need to be there, must we be there all the time?

Time-stealers are not always trivial. Some managers feel it is their moral duty to solve the problems of all who work for them. But in doing so, they will fail to make full use of others, and make life impossible for themselves. Delegation is an essential technique in both leadership and personal effectiveness.

▶ **Checkpoint 3.5**
What time-stealers do you suffer from? What can you do to avoid them?

STREAMLINING

If we are satisfied that a task is justified, the next question must be: Am I doing it in the most efficient way? It is easy to waste time visiting someone when a memo or a telephone call would have done, or writing lengthy reports when brief notes are enough.

Small details can make a considerable difference. Where and how do we keep papers and information that we need frequently? Are they easy to get when we want them? Do they get lost? On the other hand, are we keeping too much, cluttering up the system? Are our records in the most efficient form, both for entry of and access to information? Should they be held electronically or manually? Computers do not always save time. Managing information is discussed in Chapter 9.

Movement of all kinds is a frequent time waster. How often do we go out of our own work area, and where to? Could the frequency of journeys be reduced? Could our work area be better placed somewhere else, and if so where? Do we travel much off site, and if so are the journeys justified and made in the most efficient way? Car travel, for example, can waste much time even if the journey is quicker than by public transport; we can put time in a train or plane to productive use.

Some people are able to squeeze more activity into their time than others simply because they work faster. We may work faster because we have more natural aptitude; some can do a calculation in seconds that would take others many minutes. We may work faster because we have been better trained. If we are experienced at a job, we will work faster; all managers know the effect of the 'learning curve' on the speed of work. We will work faster if we are well-motivated. We will work faster when we are fresh than when we are tired. It is always worth examining our speed of work and how it might be improved.

▶ **Checkpoint 3.6**

Are you satisfied with your speed of work (a) overall, and (b) on specific tasks? If not, is there anything you can do to improve it? Are the tasks you do well-structured, or could you design them more efficiently? If so, how?

USING MARGINAL TIME

King Alfred is said to have divided each day into three equal parts; eight hours of work, eight hours of leisure and eight hours of sleep. This neat division sounds impracticable these days; there are so many things that do not quite fit; commuting, reading to the children, watching the tv weather forecast. But Alfred's approach does highlight just how many hours each day has really got, and the risk that many of them are being wasted.

There are several points at which waste may occur in a typical manager's schedule. The benefit of using public transport has already been mentioned; many managers find this valuable for keeping up with their reading. Commuting and waiting around at stations and airports can be turned into useful time. Time in hotels is often wasted, perhaps because we have not brought the necessary papers. More managers are finding the latest laptop or notebook computers, possibly combined with a modem or a portable printer, an immense help.

Depending on whether we are owls or larks, when the pressure is on we may get more done by arriving early or staying late. An hour of quiet concentration can be worth two or three disrupted by the ringing of phones and the interruptions of callers. However, as was said earlier, to come in early or stay late every day may suggest that something is wrong. The culture of some organisations pressurises managers to stay late just for the sake of it, but this is a pity. Other managers may stay late to avoid family responsibilities, but this is tragic.

39

Some managers feel the need to take work home. This is fine when we are writing an important report, completing the annual budget, handling a one-off crisis, coping with occasional backlogs or major problems. However, if we do it regularly, it also is a sign that something is wrong.

▶ **Checkpoint 3.7**
Do you regularly arrive early, stay late or take work home? If so, why? Is it really justified, or is there a better way?

Stress and health management

Management is regarded as a highly stressed occupation, with the risks for health this entails. Stress is a subjective condition, and affects each manager under different conditions, in different ways and with different results. A situation that would stress one individual stimulates another and brings the best from them.

In demanding situations, some degree of stress is helpful, even essential, to success. It sets the adrenalin flowing and gets mind and body ready for peak performance. Few managers would make good presentations, whether to their board or to key customers, unless they felt a degree of nerves, at least when starting. Few would tackle critical decisions or difficult subordinates, without the spur of at least temporary stress. But the borderline between beneficial and harmful stress is important, and it is easy to cross it.

Stress becomes harmful when it is too extreme, even in circumstances in which some stress is to be expected. The manager who is reduced to a shivering, incomprehensible wreck before a major speech or a disciplinary hearing cannot function properly. But the most damaging effects of stress occur when it is felt over the longer term, and carried into contexts in which it is out of place. If we fear coming into work not just occasionally, but every day, or lie awake worrying every night, the time has come to do something about it.

SYMPTOMS OF STRESS

- Unexplained deterioration in job performance
- Uncontrolled exhibitions of temper or emotion
- Increased and regular sick leave
- Increase in smoking
- Heavy drinking
- Regular loss of sleep or appetite

Stress that becomes chronic and serious can also affect our physical health, especially through the heart and digestive system. It may be transferred from our working to our personal life, and can affect every aspect of it, especially our relationships with partner and children.

Excessive stress may also be transferred from the personal to the working life; those who suffer problems with personal relationships, finance, the health of close family, or other areas will inevitably run the risk of lowered job performance. As managers we should remain aware of such possibilities, not only in others but in ourself.

Chronic and excessive job-related stress can be described as the result of a mismatch between job and jobholder. It may take considerable courage to face this possibility in ourself, but to do so may be far more sensible than risking physical or mental breakdown or permanent damage to relationships.

There are a number of possibilities for remedial action.

RELIEVING JOB-RELATED STRESS

- Support and counselling
- Training
- Job redesign
- Job change/rotation
- Regular exercise

SUPPORT AND COUNSELLING

In management, as in other aspects of life, a problem shared is a problem halved. The opportunity to talk problems through with someone else can often be enough to defuse situations which would otherwise deteriorate. There are a number of choices, from which most of us should be able to find a sympathetic ear and wise counsel:

- Our partner
- A colleague
- Our boss
- A human resources professional
- A career counsellor
- Our doctor

Managers need to be both on the giving and the receiving end of such opportunities. The overall culture of the organisation is important; stress problems and their symptoms should be regarded as a cue for help rather than a weakness.

TRAINING

Lack of necessary training can be a potent source of stress. All too many organisations fail to train newly-appointed supervisors and managers in the additional skills their job requires. Managers who find themselves in this position should set about managing their own bosses and obtaining the training support they need. Failing all else, study of well-chosen books such as this can provide the necessary help!

JOB REDESIGN

Excessive stress may be caused by the nature of the job. Probably the

41

commonest difficulty is an unreasonable and unpredictable mix of requirements; a job that calls for detailed attention to figures, for example, combined with irregular contacts with very senior individuals, or perhaps control of an unskilled workforce combined with the handling of customer complaints. A span of control that is too large or too varied can produce also frequently stress.

Pure quantity of work can cause stress; with the best job design, the most efficient working practices and the most talented manager, there will be a limit to the volume that can be handled.

In fact, these problems may be particularly difficult to discuss with an unhelpful boss. But if we are stressed, our job performance will suffer, and a positive discussion should help both us and our employer.

JOB CHANGE/ROTATION

42

After all other options have been considered, the need for a change of job must be faced. Perhaps the commonest situation is the skilled specialist who finds that management is not for them. Sadly, organisations are not always as responsible as they might be in helping those they have selected and promoted unsuitably.

The need to consider a change of career direction is now a more realistic option than in years gone by. It is possible to obtain counselling from professional career counsellors, either within our organisation, from our professional institution, or from outside specialists.

REGULAR EXERCISE

Many managers get little chance for balanced physical exercise in their work, and may find they have insufficient time or energy to get exercise afterwards. One or two organisations provide health suites on site, as do a few hotels. A very small number of British organisations encourage or expect their employees to join in physical exercise based on the Japanese model. For the great majority of managers, who have none of these opportunities, the discipline of regular exercise, possibly in a lunch break or before work, can help to relieve stress and maintain physical health and fitness.

▶ **Checkpoint 3.8**
Do you believe you are suffering from chronic stress? If so, have you discussed it with anyone? What further action should be taken?

Self-development

Managers owe it to themselves to ensure that they develop themselves at least as systematically as those who work with them. The subject of career planning has come to the fore in recent years, and for good reason. Two new factors have added to the need for this.

Firstly, employees no longer expect to remain with the same employer throughout their career. Most upwardly-mobile individuals can expect to change their employer on a number of occasions during their career. Indeed, many employers will expect this, and regard it as an advantage by providing greater breadth of experience.

Secondly, managers, like others, can no longer expect to learn all they need for a successful career at or near its start. Changes in technology and the marketplace and advances in knowledge make continuous updating essential. Good management practice will continue to change as a result of changed social norms, new research and a general raising of standards. Even managers whose only desire is to stay in the same place must, like the White Queen, run quite hard to do so.

43

Managers who wish to be upwardly-mobile face the need to develop themselves continually, and to plan that development as carefully as they can. Despite the flattening of management structures, it will remain true that the higher levels of management call for additional and different skills to the lower levels. We must develop not just for our present job, but for the ones to follow.

The tools of self-development will, of course, be the same as for the development of others; these are discussed in Chapter 6. We should ensure that we make appropriate use of those developmental techniques that are available to us. We should do everything practicable to plan career moves, to provide a balance of relevant experience. We should make full use of the help available from employers, professional associations and public sources in ensuring continuous professional development. Only managers who develop themselves will be able to help others develop their own skills.

▶ **Checkpoint 3.9**

What personal development activity (apart from reading this book) have you undertaken during the last six months? Have you made plans for your own career development? If so, are you acting on them? If not, when will you start?

4

Planning

> - **The need for planning**
> - **Types of plan**
> - **Factors affecting the success of a plan**
> - **The elements of a plan**

Planning is the first element of the Management Sequence, upon which the rest is based.

The need for planning

Some managers spend most of their time 'fire-fighting'; reacting to events rather than controlling them. Unplanned activities may occur in the best of organisations once in a while, as a response to unusual events; 'acts of God', as the insurance industry rather negatively calls them. But if they happen often, they are signs of poor planning. It is impossible to organise or control something that has not been planned. The start of every act of management must be the making of a plan.

Plans may be extremely simple:

> *I plan to visit head office in London on Tuesday morning.*

Or they may be immensely complex:

> *To build and commission a production facility for the new product range.*

Plans should exist for everything a manager does. Simple plans may be only in the manager's head, but plans of any complexity, that affect more than one or two people, or that reach more than a short time ahead, are always best written down.

► **Checkpoint 4.1**
Do you consider short-term plans when undertaking any non-routine activity?
Are your plans written down in any form? What current short- and long-term
plans do you have in your job?

Types of plan

Plans are made at every level within an organisation, and everyone will
be affected by plans made by others. Any function or unit may (and
should) plan. The main kinds of plan are:

- Corporate or strategic plans
- Business plans
- Operational plans
- Project plans

CORPORATE PLANS

Corporate or strategic plans are, as the name implies, made for a whole
organisation. They should be the basis for all that the organisation seeks
to do during the period covered. Such plans are usually fairly long-term,
typically covering a minimum of one year and possibly as much as five
years ahead. Many organisations 'roll their plans forward' annually;
that is, add a further year in place of the one just ended, and revise and
update the plan for the intervening years. They will cover every aspect of
the operation; indeed, one of the most valuable features of corporate
plans is the linkage that they provide between different functions and
activities.

Most organisations make corporate plans 'top down', but an increasing
number involve managers at every level, and may work 'bottom up',
synthesising their plan from the inputs of each individual unit.

BUSINESS PLANS

Many smaller organisations will formulate a 'business plan'. This is of
particular importance when seeking to raise finance, and is expected by
bank managers and others in this field. This kind of business plan is, in
effect, a corporate plan under another name. Within larger organisations, business plans may be produced for new products or specific
projects.

45

OPERATIONAL PLANS

The description 'operational planning' is given to the day-to day and month by month planning of managers in every area. As such, it is the kind of planning we will most frequently do. Often, it will be done in our head, or be no more than a simple list on the back of an envelope. But we should always do it.

How far ahead we can sensibly plan – our 'planning horizon' – will depend on factors such as how routine our operation is and the nature of the work that our customers (internal or external) require. If the work consists of a small number of major and unique assignments (such as major design projects), our planning will be quite different from what will be needed to plan for a large number of similar jobs (such as serving retail customers). This is touched on again in Chapter 7.

A plan may be handed down from higher management or from other departments, but in accepting it, managers will accept responsibility for its fulfilment. We owe it to ourselves and our unit to be satisfied that it is properly constructed and achievable. Nothing is gained by accepting what appear to be impossible objectives. In the last analysis, we may feel the need to put our reservations on record; clearly this should not happen often, but it is preferable to accepting responsibility for a plan which will not work.

PROJECT PLANS

Projects are activities outside the everyday work of an organisation that are more or less self-contained. These have been described as 'instruments of change'. Every project should be planned, whatever its size. Typical projects might include:

- Building a new office or factory
- Introduction of a new product
- Introduction of new machinery
- Major changes to working methods
- Introduction of a new corporate image

Project planning and management is an area of management with its own skills and problems. Anyone involved in the planning of a major project should obtain specialised guidance from the many books and courses available.

▶ **Checkpoint 4.2**

What levels of planning do you get involved in? Does your organisation make its corporate plans 'bottom up' or 'top down'? Have you ever been involved in a major project?

Factors affecting the likely success of a plan

Few plans work out exactly as made, and, as Rabbie Burns pointed out plans will, 'gang aft agley'. In making our plan, be it simple or complex, we will need to consider the problems that might beset it, and how they can be avoided.

The likely success of a plan will depend on factors including:

- Complexity
- Planning horizon
- Number of individuals and organisations involved
- Sensitivity to uncontrollable factors

THE COMPLEXITY

The more complex a plan is, the more chance there must be of its going wrong. Simplicity in planning is a virtue in its own right.

THE PLANNING HORIZON

The further ahead a plan reaches, the more problems it is likely to encounter. Something planned for this afternoon is more likely, other factors being equal, to go according to the plan than the same activity planned for an afternoon in six months' time. All forecasts become less reliable the further ahead they reach.

THE NUMBER OF INDIVIDUALS AND ORGANISATIONS INVOLVED

The more people, departments, or organisations that have a part in our plan, the more possibilities exist for failure. If we are carrying it out ourself from start to finish we should have the knowledge and motivation to succeed; others may not have so much of either. The more individuals or units involved, the greater the need for organisation and co-ordination and the harder control will be.

THE SENSITIVITY OF THE PLAN TO UNCONTROLLABLE FACTORS

However well we plan, there will always be risks from factors outside our control. We may suffer from 'acts of God'; earthquake, storm or tempest. There may be sudden economic or political changes; a rise in interest rates, for example, or a change in government. International problems; wars, trade embargoes, exchange-rate fluctuations and so on may arise. Our boss may return from his annual holiday or wake up in a bad mood.

These factors may destroy a plan (if the boss says 'No', for example), or they may have only a small effect (if, for example, the rise in interest rates only increases the cost of borrowing a small proportion of the capital for our plan). The more deeply the plan would be affected, the greater its sensitivity to that factor.

▶ **Checkpoint 4.3**

Examine a current plan with which you are involved. To what extent might its success be in danger from the factors listed in this section? Can the dangers be reduced?

THE ELEMENTS OF A PLAN

However simple, every plan should have six elements, even if only in the manager's mind:

- Aim
- Objectives
- Activities
- Schedule
- Performance indicators
- Protection

Every plan must have an *aim*; a statement of what it is intended to achieve. For example:

> *The aim is to have the new offices fully equipped, staffed and in full operation by the end of November.*

An accurate, written description of the aim of is always worth producing before any further work proceeds, even if the plan is simple. Writing it down helps to clarify our thinking and strengthen our commitment. If the plan involves a number of people, a written aim is essential, to ensure that everyone is pulling in the same direction.

Objectives are more detailed statements about how the aim will be achieved. For example, related to the aim suggested in the previous section, our objectives may be:

- To limit overall expenditure to £50,000
- Not to disturb the working of other offices and departments
- To ensure that the IT equipment installed is compatible with other company systems and that its installation does not disturb their working
- To ensure all staff are recruited (or transferred) and physically in post at least two weeks before opening to allow for familiarisation and training and so on.

Unless our plan is to lie doggo and show masterly inactivity, every plan must have one or more *activities*. These are the steps or elements in a plan necessary to achieve its aim and objectives. A simple plan may have only one or two activities, but, we must consider each from four points of view:

- *Responsibility*: the responsibility for ensuring the activity is properly carried out must always be made clear to everyone involved
- *Sequence*: must some activities be completed before others can start?
- *Float time*: do individual activities have any slack? What would be the effect on other activities if they overran?
- *Resourcing*: will the resources of cash, manpower be available when required? Is there a potential conflict (e.g. someone required in two places at once)?

A complex plan may need to be broken down into a large number of activities; hundreds or even thousands. Such a plan will invariably be constructed in the form of a network showing the logical connections between each activity, and which must be completed before others can start. The network will also include information on the planned time to be taken by each activity, from which the amount of float time can be calculated. Those activities which have no float time – that is, whose delay would delay final completion of the plan – are said to be on the *critical path*. For this reason, network analysis is sometimes known as critical path analysis, or CPA.

For large plans of this kind the manager will need computing power and the support of experts in project management and related techniques.

49

Fig. 4.1 Network-making a cup of tea

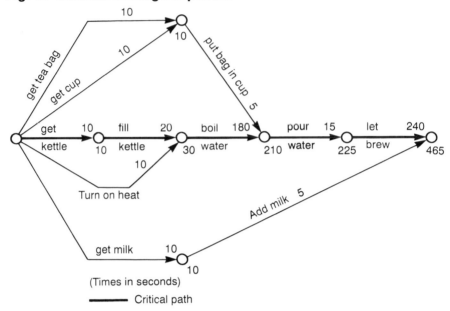

(Times in seconds)

—— Critical path

However, the concept of network planning is elegant and helpful, and managers who have mastered it can use it themselves as a tool of any sort of planning. There are several books and courses available on the subject.

Simple plans can sensibly be broken down into a number of activities that can be handled by the individual manager on one sheet of paper:

Aim and objectives: to get cash
Activities: 1 Go to bank
                2 Insert cashpoint card in machine
                3 Enter number and amount
                4 Withdraw card and cash
                5 Return home

Every plan should have its *schedule* or timescale. Indeed, lack of a timescale is probably the commonest failure in day-to-day, simple planning. The second commonest is to be over-optimistic in setting the timescale.

The schedules for plans with a small number of activities can be made up readily by the manager and staff concerned. Schedules for complex plans will be derived from the network.

Once a schedule has been produced, by whatever method, it can be represented by a bar or Gantt chart, in which each activity is represented by a bar plotted against a time scale (see Figure 4.2).

Fig. 4.2 A Gantt chart

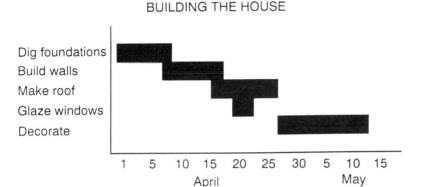

BUILDING THE HOUSE

Performance indicators/standards are measures to indicate whether work is proceeding according to the plan. They may also be called 'targets' or 'goals'.

PERFORMANCE INDICATORS CAN BE BASED ON:	
■ Deadlines/schedule	■ Quality/reject levels
■ Budget projections	■ Market research ratings
■ Cash flow	■ Success rates
■ Stock/consumables usage	■ Accident/safety record
■ Sales targets	■ Customer complaints
■ Production/delivery targets	

Effective control will require that data should be collected as soon as work starts. Quantitative data is always much easier to use, but may be difficult, or even impossible, to obtain. In some situations, qualitative data, in the form of verbal reports, may be all that is available. Where this is the case, it is essential to try to eliminate bias and unsubstantiated opinion, which can cause particular problems when human behaviour is being reported.

Data collection may be at regular intervals; if so, it will be important to decide what these should be. Commonly data will be collected frequently after a new process has been established, or when problems are being experienced, and less frequently as successful experience is built up. It is a classic fault of bureaucracy to collect too much data too frequently, and the production of historic reports can become a drag on both productivity and innovation.

In some situations it is more helpful to collect data at random intervals, possibly as part of occasional inspection.

Data may be collected manually, or automatically. The growth of information technology and instrumentation has made automatic collection of data practical in many situations. The subject of information management is discussed in Chapter 9.

▶ **Checkpoint 4.4**

What performance indicators are used to assess work in your area? How is data collected against these, and how frequently? Is too much data collected? Are too many reports called for? If so why, and by whom? Is this phase effective, and how might it be made more effective?

The budget is one of the commonest and most important performance indicators. A budget indicating the amount of money allocated to a plan, item by item, is generally regarded as essential, both to the initial making and approval of the plan and subsequent control of its progress. If the help of a management accountant is available, we should use it. However, managers cannot escape the need for a proper understanding of the financial picture, how figures are made up and what they mean. Budgetary procedures and the interpretation of other financial data are discussed in Chapter 10.

Apart from the total amount of money spent under different categories, the timing of expenditure and income is often critical – what is known as the cash flow. This is also discussed in Chapter 10.

Having made a plan, the effective manager will want to do whatever he can to protect it and ensure that it works as it should. *Plan protection* is not always properly considered, but is of immense value and well worth any time taken.

Plan protection starts most logically by considering each main activity, and asking the following questions:

- What might go wrong with this activity?
- For each thing that might go wrong,
  - (a) How serious would it be if it did go wrong?
  - (b) How likely is it to go wrong in this way?
- For each high threat problem (both serious and likely) consider:
  - (a) Can we prevent this happening? If so how and is it realistic?
  - (b) If this does happen, what contingency plan can we set up to limit the harm?
  - (c) What will trigger implementation of the contingency?
  - (d) If the contingency plan does not work, can we accept the damage that would be caused to the plan? If not, we may have to re-plan without this element.

▶ **Checkpoint 4.6**

Have you ever set about methodical protection of a plan you have made, including contingency plans? If so, did it help? If not, do you feel it could have been useful? In either case, experiment by setting protection for the next plan with which you are involved.

5

Organisation

- Shorter-term organisation
- The need for organisation structure
- The elements of organisation structure
- Reporting relationships
- Types of organisation structure
- A checklist for organisational effectiveness

Organisation is the act of ensuring that the resources needed to implement the plan will be available as and when needed, and that the various activities will contribute to, and not interfere with, each other. This is the second phase of the Management Sequence, following the making of a plan. As with planning, organising may be anything from a routine action taking a couple of minutes to a complicated, long-lasting structure. This will depend on the size, importance, familiarity and complexity of what is to be done. But whichever it is, organisation is an essential element of the act of managing.

Shorter-term organisation

In the shorter term, organising is a highly dynamic activity. It involves mobilising the necessary resources and allocating them to their place in the plan. The human resource will, as always in management, be crucial, and everyone involved will need to be briefed on their role. There may be a need for training – possibly for practice or rehearsal. Organising will call for many management skills, including communication, motivation, problem-solving and decision-making.

Co-ordination is a vital ingredient in this phase. There is little virtue in delivering the shovels to point A next week if the load of manure was delivered to point B yesterday and the shovellers have just started a fortnight's annual holiday.

CHECKLISTS

Many practising managers find checklists of great value when organising, and prepare lists for situations they are likely to meet. Many such management checklists are available in book or pamphlet form (see box for an example checklist).

SETTING UP A MEETING

- Check available dates and times with all participants
- Book suitable room for chosen date and times (start and finish)
- Produce and circulate calling notice with:
  - ★ date
  - ★ place
  - ★ map/car parking/public transport details [if necessary]
  - ★ start and expected finish times
  - ★ list of participants
  - ★ agenda
- Arrange for appropriate refreshments
- Ensure necessary equipment is available:
  - ★ chairs
  - ★ tables/desks
  - ★ flipcharts/stands/markers
  - ★ overhead projector/screen/acetates
  - ★ notepads/pencils/glasses/water

55

PROCEDURES

Frequently-repeated tasks benefit from being organised in the form of a written-up procedure. The act of producing such a procedure offers an opportunity to check whether the method being followed is the best. Once produced, the procedure will provide guidance on what should be done both for operative and manager. It can also help in job evaluation, recruitment and the training of staff. The adoption of quality control standards such as BS 5750 and ISO 9000 requires that procedures should be fully written up.

Over-rigid procedures can become bureaucratic, and hinder rather than help. We must ensure that all our procedures are flexible enough to allow for differing circumstances, and that someone is always accessible with sufficient authority to adapt them intelligently. The needs of customers should always come before blind adherence to a procedure.

▶ **Checkpoint 5.1**

Do you use checklists to help organise? If not, are there activities in which they would help? Does your organisation have many formalised procedures? Do those that exist help or hinder the organising phase of management? How might they be made more helpful?

The need for organisation structure

56

Organising on-going activities will require not only procedures but structures. Any group of people that remain together for any length of time will naturally develop a structure. If the group has a common purpose, it will develop a clearer and stronger structure. Consider the following groups:

- A family
- The residents of Brookside
- Your local cricket club
- A growing engineering company with 25 employees
- A chamber cf 25 barristers
- British Rail
- An army brigade

The structures of each differs for a number of reasons.

Time is an important factor; a group that remains together for any appreciable length of time, such as a neighbourhood, will develop its own structure of relationships between the members, simply because they remain together; individuals will fit into habitual roles and develop expectations as to each other's behaviour.

The nature and strength of a group structure will depend on the existence of a common *purpose* that is shared between members. The clearer the purpose, the clearer the structure. The extent to which a family has structure will depend partly on the age of its members and whether they feel a common purpose, or merely live under one roof for convenience.

The cricket club structure is likely to be simple and flexible, as the overall purpose may be seen differently by different members.

The nature and rigidity of a structure will also vary according to the *size* of the group. In general, the larger a group, the more rigid its structure must be to ensure cohesion of its efforts towards its goals. The engineering company of 25 employees would probably be on the borderline. When it was smaller, it could probably function well with a high degree of flexibility; people could 'muck in' as the need arose. Much larger, and its employees could not function without defined roles and relationships. British Rail and the brigade are of a size that makes a clear, rigid structure essential.

How rigidly the roles and relationships are defined will also depend on a range of other factors including the variety of skills involved, the nature of the work and the style of its managers. It is probable that the structure of the chamber of barristers would be simpler and less rigid than that of the engineering company.

57

PROBLEMS WITH ORGANISATION STRUCTURES

Smaller organisations will usually have fairly simple and informal structures, based on the changing needs and personalities. For them, organisation structure may not usually be a problem, although periods of change, especially growth or the loss of senior people, may precipitate a crisis. Even in the smallest organisations the principles of sound structure hold good, and we neglect them at our peril.

Structure will often be a problem for larger organisations. Many have just grown, like Topsy. It is common for structures to develop to suit individual managers and their personal background, interests, relationships and power-bases. This is inevitable, and most people would say it is right, at least up to a point. However, powerful, senior managers can distort structures too far in their own interests, so that the organisation ceases to function efficiently. Even when this is not the case, individuals leave, or change jobs, and this can result in an organisation structure that offers the worst of all worlds.

Any organisation in which sections, departments, functions, factories, branches, site divisions or other units are not well co-ordinated, any organisation that does not respond to customers' needs, does not communicate effectively, or that has conflicting chains of command, has structural problems.

Structures take on a life of their own as time goes on. The structures of religious and state institutions, older colleges, schools, learned bodies and regiments may change little over decades – even centuries. What were originally meaningful actions are frequently petrified into ceremonies and traditions. They may gradually fail to adapt to external changes. Whilst few commercial organisations exist long enough for such changes to go far, they may start. Rigidity can become so great that the organisation becomes insufficiently responsive and dies from what Professor Parkinson calls 'injelititis'.

▶ **Checkpoint 5.2**

How rigid and formal is the structure of your own organisation? What factors have made it what it is? Is the existing structure effective? If not, what changes do you think should be made?

The elements of organisation structure

To work, every organisation structure must define the roles within it. The definition must make clear:

- Functional specialisations
- Job definition
- Levels of authority
- Reporting relationships

Each of these is now considered.

FUNCTIONAL SPECIALISATION

Functional specialisation allows people to specialise in a limited range of work, thus using their natural skills and interests to best advantage, and developing greater expertise. It also helps the smooth functioning of the organisation, as both internal and external customers know who is best able to meet their needs.

A one-person organisation must inevitably combine most of the functions. Those beyond the skill (or available time) of the individual – typically such functions as legal and accountancy – can be bought in. As organisations grow, most will become more functionalised. The first split is often between the essential functions of marketing and production.

Individuals who are interested and skilful in one area are often less interested and skilful in the other. Few craft workers are good at selling their artifacts, and few salespeople are motivated by the problems and techniques of designing and making things.

As the organisation grows, other functional splits will occur. The next may be between research and development (R&D) and production; the person who has the knowledge and imagination to create products may not be interested or skilled in the dirty business of actually making them. As the number of employees increases, a human resources specialist will be needed; an in-house accountant may be recruited; sales may split from marketing, and so on.

The principle functional divisions, which exist in most organisations of any size, are between:

Marketing/sales: establishes the potential and actual market for the organisation's present and possible future products or services, and presents and sells them.

Design/engineering/research and development: designs and develops new products or services, and ensures that existing ones perform properly.

Production/manufacturing: actually produces the product or service of the organisation, or buys it or component parts of it from outside.

Finance/accountancy: monitors expenditure, income, capital requirements and cash flow. It must meet the needs of company and taxation law, of the owners of the business and of managers.

Personnel/human resources: supports managers in the use of people, their development and training and in industrial relations matters.

As growth continues, even more specialised functions may become necessary. Some, such as the company secretariat, may be added as a self-contained function at the highest level in the organisation. Others may be formed as a further split of one of the existing functions; production engineering may be split from the production function, for example, or industrial relations from personnel.

A functionalised organisation structure has clear advantages, and is generally felt to be essential. However, there are also disadvantages, such as the conflict and rivalry that can grow between functional empires; complex lines of communication, and limitations on individuals' career development.

► **Checkpoint 5.3**

How extensive is the functional split within your own organisation? Does it work well, or would there be benefit from its being more or less functionalised? What drawbacks, if any, has the organisation suffered from functionalisation?

JOB DEFINITION

It is essential, both for members of an organisation and for its external customers, to know who does what job. Job titles help, especially if they are reasonably precise and generally understood; 'computer programmer', 'receptionist', 'director of finance' and so on. However, many job titles are vague, specialist or used in a variety of ways: 'administration manager', 'liaison officer', 'value engineer', 'production co-ordinator'.

For detailed purposes, written descriptions of duties and responsibilities are essential. Most organisations, except for the very smallest, produce job descriptions for all posts as a matter of course. Producing descriptions helps to avoid duplication and to ensure that everything is covered. When completed, they are useful in filling vacancies, fixing levels of remuneration and analysing training needs.

However, written job descriptions also have drawbacks. They may become too restricting, especially in an organisation that is growing or changing rapidly. They may not take account of the strengths and interests of individual job holders, and can limit the use the organisation makes of its people. If morale is low, or industrial relations difficulties arise, they can be used as a weapon ('That's not in my job description.') They can get out of date quite rapidly.

A few organisations encourage job-holders to write their own job descriptions. Without co-ordination, such an approach could lead to problems, but it can also help the better use of individual potential. We may feel it possible to experiment, in the right circumstances.

► **Checkpoint 5.4**

Do you have a written job description? Who wrote it, and when? Does it really describe what you do? Has it proved a benefit or a drawback to you or your organisation?

LEVELS OF AUTHORITY

If anyone within an organisation could issue any kind of order – the doubling of salaries, for example, or the buying of a new office block – it would be a recipe for immediate chaos. Whether inside or outside an organisation, we must know who has authority to issue instructions, and what restrictions there are (if any) on that authority.

Devolution of authority is simplest in financial matters, and many organisations give progressively less spending authority to each tier of management.

In practice, managers are often unsure how far their authority stretches. All too often, they do not find out until too late, when they fail to receive support for a controversial decision. As effective managers we will need to establish as clearly as possible what the limits of our authority are. We will also make as clear as possible the authority we allow to those who work for us.

In formal, bureaucratic organisations, authority will go with the job. In less formal organisations, the process of handing over authority is often a slow one, developing as the relationship between individuals develops, and depending on the degree of personal trust. In such organisations, we will need to avoid the twin dangers of keeping too much authority to ourself, or giving away more than we intend and having to countermand the decisions of our people.

Responsibility and authority must be devolved equally. A manager responsible for setting up a computerised accountancy system, but without authority to choose equipment, select staff or instruct other managers how to operate the system will have problems.

► **Checkpoint 5.5**
Do you know the limits of your authority, especially in financial and personnel matters? Have you ever experienced problems, either by being accused of overstepping your authority or failing to make full use of it? Does your authority match your responsibility, and if not, in what ways?

Reporting relationships

Reporting relationships are the lines of authority and formal communication within an organisation structure.

They are described as of four kinds:

- Line
- Functional
- Staff
- Lateral

Line relationships are those by which direct authority and control is exercised – the 'hire and fire' or 'pay and rations' relationship. They link a manager with his or her subordinates, and are the channels by which instructions are formally given.

The *span of control* is the number of people with direct line responsibility to one manager. If a span of control is too wide, managers will not have the time – possibly not the expertise – to cope. There must clearly be a limit. On the other hand, if too narrow a span of control is chosen, individuals will feel they are over-supervised and prevented from using initiative. There will need to be too many levels, long lines of communication and excessive numbers of middle managers.

There can be no rigid rule as to how many people should report directly. The factors involved include:

- *The variety of work* performed by subordinates. If all subordinates are doing the same or similar work, the span of control can be wider.
- *The geographical spread.* If all subordinates work in the same location the span can be wider than if they are travelling or widely dispersed.
- *The nature of the work.* The more routine the work performed by subordinates, the wider the span can be.
- *The maturity of the team.* The more mature the team and the individuals in it, the wider the span of control can be.

In the most favourable circumstances, such as an office or machine shop where well-trained individuals are performing simple, identical, routine tasks, the maximum span of control will be about 30. In the least favourable, such as a new team of staff each performing different, complex tasks at separate locations, the maximum span of control might be as little as three. In average circumstances, five or six is felt to be a workable span.

Functional relationships are those between senior and junior personnel within the same function who have another line relationship. A works accountant, for example, is likely to have a functional relationship with the company accountant, but a line relationship with his or her works manager. The functional or professional standards and procedures will be laid down and monitored through the functional relationship. Functional relationships may be called 'dotted lines' because they are usually shown in this way on organisation charts.

Staff relationships are those in which one individual (e.g. a secretary or personal assistant) works exclusively for another and acts as a chain of communication and transmission of their authority. Such relationships are usually confined to the highest level in an organisation, especially in the public sector (e.g. the private office of a government minister).

Lateral relationships are those necessary by way of regular business between colleagues of approximately the same level. Thus the sales and marketing managers of an organisation will need a strong lateral relationship involving particularly close and continuing communication.

Formal relationships and channels of communication may often be less important and less efficient than informal contacts between colleagues who know each other and work well together. They probably contribute more to managerial effectiveness than the relationships depicted on organisation charts, essential as the latter are. These individual networks – the 'grapevine' – are also mentioned in Chapter 8.

63

▶ **Checkpoint 5.6**

Are you clear who your own line manager is? Do you also have a functional boss, and if so, does this cause any problems? For how many subordinates do you have line responsibility? Is it a workable number? If not, why not?

TYPES OF ORGANISATION STRUCTURE

Piecing together the elements we have discussed, it is possible to identify the commonest types of organisation structure.

Centralised structures

This form of organisation is sometimes called the 'line and staff' or 'bureaucratic' structure. Until fairly recently, it was almost universal for organisations of any size, and it remains common, especially in the public sector. In centralised organisations the bulk of authority and decision-making lies with headquarters. All the principal functions will be represented in the headquarters unit. Management control will be exercised by a reporting structure of line and functional relationships, as described above. Managers outside this unit are required to act in accordance with the rules and procedures that it has laid down, often in comprehensive detail.

An organisation chart for such a structure is:

Chart A Centralised organisation structure

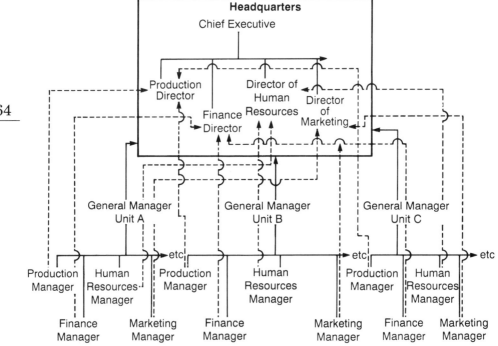

This type of structure offers a number of advantages, and has proved of lasting value to many organisations.

ADVANTAGES OF CENTRALISED STRUCTURES

- A clear chain of command that is readily understandable both inside and outside the organisation.

- A firm and lasting control structure capable of coping with a wide variety of circumstances.

- Optimal spans of control and levels of authority.

Organisations in which uniformity is essential, for operational, commercial, social or legal reasons find this form of structure appropriate. An army, for example, must have a unified command structure. Civil service departments must operate the same procedures throughout the country. A railway can only operate effectively if its equipment and operating methods are standardised. A multinational oil company must have a strong corporate image and centralised distribution and pricing.

Centralised structures also have generally-recognised problems and characteristic drawbacks.

DISADVANTAGES OF CENTRALISED STRUCTURES

- Long chains of command through which information and decisions can become distorted and delayed. (The 'send three and fourpence – we're going to a dance' syndrome.)

- Departments and functions may lose direct linkage with the product or service for which the whole organisation exists and develop a life of their own.

- Unresponsive, both to local circumstances, and changes over time. They can fail to detect the need for change, and be highly resistant to the need to adapt. They rarely support innovation and creativity.

- Frequent conflict between line and functional command. Split or uncertain loyalties can cause major problems.

- Empire-building by functions and departments can occur and be difficult to detect and control.

- Reduced initiative-taking and decision-making role of managers, who may have their freedom of action so restricted that they become no more than routine administrators.

65

For these reasons, such structures have in many cases been abandoned or radically changed, especially within the private sector, and a degree of decentralisation has been introduced.

DECENTRALISED STRUCTURES

Decentralised organisation structures aim to place authority at the lowest practicable level. This will involve reducing the role of organisational headquarters and devolving authority to operating units. Within each unit the structure will usually be of the line and staff type, but with no functional reporting and limited line reporting to headquarters. This approach can be applied by decentralising to separate geographical, product or functional units. Authority may be devolved to factories, product divisions, countries or regions, individual or ranges of products or specific functions.

Control will be maintained through a range of performance criteria for each units. In the extreme case, it will be confined to little more than the 'bottom line': overall financial performance. Parts of the organisation may even be established as separate companies owned by the parent group.

The same structure can result when a group is formed by takeover of a number of smaller companies, but allows each to continue operating with only loose, overall control.

<u>66</u>   An organisation chart for a decentralised structure is:

Chart B Decentralised organisation structure

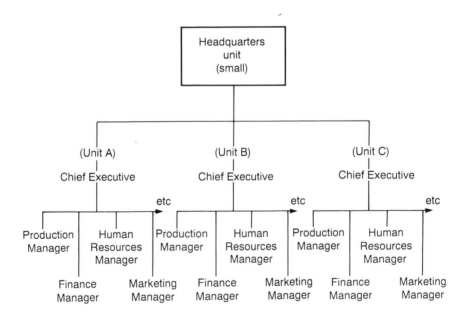

This approach has many demonstrated advantages.

ADVANTAGES OF DECENTRALISED STRUCTURES

- Managers are encouraged to display initiative and responsibility.
- Clear performance criteria for operating units.
- Short and responsive chains of command.
- Flexibility to change.

There are also, however, a number of problems to be overcome.

DISADVANTAGES OF DECENTRALISED STRUCTURES

- The difficulty, in some organisations, of making a meaningful, workable split between operations.
- The problems of preserving a recognisable image in the marketplace.
- Possible industrial relations problems (e.g. a change to local negotiation of pay and conditions).
- The limiting of career development opportunities for professional and managerial staff.
- The line/functional conflict may still exist, even if on a smaller scale.

67

MATRIX OR PROJECT-BASED STRUCTURES

In some organisations, there has been a move towards 'matrix', or project-based structures. Matrix structures seek to combine the advantages of both line and staff and decentralised structures. Project managers are appointed to establish and lead cross-functional teams responsible for work on a specific project or product. The teams may exist for months, possibly years, but will be dissolved and changed as needs change. Within the teams, authority will be exercised by the project manager, although functional authority will usually also continue to be exercised.

Chart C Matrix organisation structure

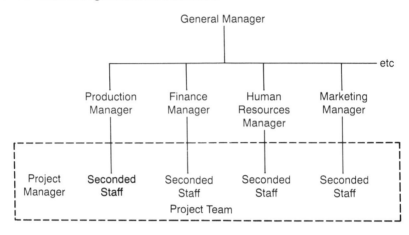

Matrix structures have some advantages.

ADVANTAGES OF MATRIX STRUCTURES

■ Responsiveness.

■ Strong loyalty and commitment generated to specific projects.

■ Flexibility to changed needs.

They also have a number of drawbacks.

DISADVANTAGES OF MATRIX STRUCTURES

■ Conflicts for scarce resources may become bitter and require high-level resolution.

■ Loyalty to the project team may become too strong and conflict with other organisational needs.

FLAT STRUCTURES

A few, exceptional, organisations may choose a completely flat, one-level structure, in which each individual has equal authority. In case of conflict, or for decisions above a certain level, only the group as a whole can decide and act. This structure may be used within some professional practices, partnerships, small co-operatives and informal groups.

Most structures can be said to have 'flat authority' at the top level, in that the ultimate decision-making power is likely to lie with a council, board or committee. However, for all levels below this, such a structure would be too cumbersome, too slow to respond and too liable to misuse.

In recent years there has been a thrust towards flatter organisation structures, with a minimum of levels of authority, of whatever type. There are several benefits to this approach.

ADVANTAGES OF FLAT STRUCTURES

- Short chains of command.
- Responsiveness.
- Greater authority at operating level.
- Greater job satisfaction.
- Reduced cost of middle management.

There are also some drawbacks.

DISADVANTAGES OF FLAT STRUCTURES

- Poor promotional prospects.
- Wide spans of control.

This process has been given the painful-sounding description 'delayering', and is, in fact, often very painful for the middle managers who lose their jobs in consequence.

▶ **Checkpoint 5.7**
How would you describe the structure of your organisation? Does it work well? If not, how could it be improved?

Checklist of organisational effectiveness

Organisation structure is a classic field for consultants, many of whom have made fortunes out of recommending changes to whatever structure they find. But it is also an area in which managers can, with the necessary authority, do much to help themselves. Here is a checklist for organisational effectiveness in your own area:

- Is decision-making, quick, effective and consistent?
- Do people at every level understand what is expected of them?
- Do channels of communication work quickly and accurately in all directions?
- Are there inter-departmental conflicts or rivalries?
- Does the organisation and all parts of it respond rapidly and appropriately to the need for change?
- Are people at every level and in all functions fully aware of, and motivated by, the need to satisfy the organisation's customers?
- Is there too much internal paperwork and too many reports?
- Are there too many committees, working parties and time-consuming and unproductive internal meetings?
- Are there too many chiefs and not enough Indians?
- Is morale good, both overall and in all parts of the organisation?

► **Checkpoint 5.7**
How effective is the organisation structure within your own operation?

Managing human resources

> ■ **The main aspects of the human resource**
> ■ **Selection and recruitment**
> ■ **Performance appraisal**
> ■ **Counselling**
> ■ **Individual development and training**
> ■ **Discipline**

Because management means 'achieving objectives through people', effective people management lies at the heart of the management task. To a large degree, people management is the same as leadership; this was discussed in Chapter 2. To some extent, people management is a matter of specialist administration; payment-by-results schemes, job grading, wages administration, documentation and so on; these are outside the scope of this book. Between people management and leadership lies a third area which is the responsibility of managers, but which is not an element of leadership as such, and in which managers work closely with human resources professionals. We can call it *human resource development*. Each element in human resource development requires the use of specific skills and techniques which managers may not use frequently, but when they are called for, are of great importance. It is this area which is the subject of this chapter.

The main aspects of the human resource

Before looking at the main elements of human resource development, it is helpful to review the main ways in which people are, in fact, a resource for the manager.

There are three main aspects:

- Labour
- Skill
- Knowledge

LABOUR

People can be regarded purely as units of labour – 'hands'. At first sight this view may appear somewhat old-fashioned, but there is nothing wrong with it. In any operation the number of people engaged may be right, too few or too many. This will be a recurring and important question in the manager's mind.

The work measurement techniques of work study and organisation and methods (O&M) offer some help in this area, and are mentioned in more detail in Chapter 7. In general, the more skilled the work, the harder it is to measure. Moreover, Professor Parkinson's famous law ('work expands to fill the time available for its completion') will operate remorselessly at every level. At the end of the day, we will often have little but our own judgement, experience and instinct to guide us.

SKILL

People are also a resource by virtue of the skills they possess or can develop. It will not help to recruit a labourer, for example, if our need is for a skilled sheet metal worker, or a copy typist if we need a computer programmer.

Many businesses rely for their success more on the skills of one or two individuals than any other factor. The growth of most successful organisations is based, at least in the early period, on the skill and character of their founder. Many organisations have been transformed (for better or worse) by the skills of a new chief executive, chairman or managing director. But the same can be true at any level and in almost any function. A single brilliant engineer, salesperson, craftsman, or financier can be central to success. The ability to recognise and develop people's skills is one of the most important skills a manager can possess.

KNOWLEDGE

The people resource also includes the knowledge they possess. As the sheer volume of knowledge and the power of information technology grow, so the value of the knowledge of individuals becomes less crucial. It is now often more important to know where to get knowledge than actually to possess it. However, there remain at least two areas in which individual knowledge remains invaluable: history and contacts.

Henry Ford said history was bunk, but he was wrong. Without a knowledge of the past, we are in continual danger of spending time and effort re-inventing the wheel. Much management effort is wasted in most organisations in this way.

Personal contacts are even more important. There are few truer sayings in management than:

> *It's not what you know, but who you know.*

Apart from the advantages in selling, many a tricky management problem has been solved quickly and easily by a personal contact. A quick word with an old pal is usually infinitely more effective than hours of laboured communication through the official channels. As managers, one of our most powerful weapons will be extensive personal networks both inside and outside the organisation; we should keep such networks in good repair.

Much of the knowledge and skill of individuals often remains untapped. Hierarchical and bureaucratic styles of management, in particular, restrict the contribution of individuals. But if we are personally secure and humble enough to realise the limitations of our own knowledge and the value of others' knowledge, we will reap a big harvest. The reservoir of knowledge, skill and commitment available at every level is one of the greatest resources open to us.

▶ **Checkpoint 6.1**
Name one or two individuals who are crucial to the success of your organisation. What is so important about their contribution? What more might they, or others, contribute, given the opportunity?

Selection and recruitment

Successful development of the human resource begins with choosing the right people to work with us. Success here can mean success for our whole operation; failure can mean disaster.

Recruitment can be an expensive process, especially at senior level. Direct costs can include advertising, agency or consultancy fees and a candidate's travel expenses. Indirect costs will include the time spent by managers and personnel advisers; reduced output, errors and corrections by the person selected during their 'learning curve'; it may include loss of customer goodwill and damage to team morale. If a really bad choice is made, these effects could be ruinous. If, on the other hand, we fail to spot a winner, it may damage our competitive position; such a person is sure to be spotted by a rival, who will then reap the benefits of their contribution. Recruitment can be time-consuming, but most managers feel that it is time that must be expended.

Filling a vacancy is a two-way process; it is as important for the candidate to be satisfied with the employer as for the employer to be satisfied with the candidate. If the candidate is misled, or misunderstands the nature of the job or the organisation, the damage will be just as serious as if the employer is misled, or misunderstands what the candidate has to offer. As recruiters, we must resist the temptation to place ourselves in positions of god-like power. Rather, we should adopt the position of one partner in a process which can easily go wrong and is of the great importance to both.

The process of selection is not, and never can be, exact. The fascination some people have for tests (whether psychometric, handwriting or astrological) is an indication of the wish for an infallible method of predicting job performance, but there can be no such thing. There can never be a means of looking into the future and seeing whether an individual will be motivated to exercise their skills, become fully committed to the organisation and the team, work harmoniously with their new manager and achieve the objectives set for them. At best, good testing can limit the field for error. If we want someone who can drive an HGV, speak fluent business French, or programme in Basic, we can test and find out the candidate's skills in the appropriate area. In most cases, the best predictor of the candidate's likely job performance will be the systematic evaluation of his or her past achievements.

Effective personnel selection must include a number of elements.

ESSENTIAL ELEMENTS OF SELECTION

The job description

- The person profile.
- The advertisement.
- Administration.
- Interviewing.

THE JOB DESCRIPTION

The clearer we can be about what we are looking for, the more chance we will have of finding it. To attempt to fill a vacancy without this is like playing a game of blind man's buff.

The first question must always be: 'Is there really a post to be filled?' The fact that the post exists does not prove that it needs to exist; indeed, if it has fallen vacant that provides an opportunity to abolish it; we may decide to combine its duties with those of other posts, or hold it vacant until circumstances change.

Having satisfied ourself that the post should be filled, we must establish exactly what the duties of its occupant are. Most medium- and larger-sized organisations have written job descriptions. However, they can only be a starting point; we will need to ensure that the job description is up-to-date. The duties may have changed; they may need to be shared differently between posts; the existing grade or salary may no longer be appropriate.

THE PERSON PROFILE

From a sound job description, we will need to consider the characteristics of the person who could successfully fill it. There are one or two traps here.

The first trap is the temptation to base our thinking too closely on the previous occupant. We may seek a carbon copy of them, or if they were a failure, an opposite. We must resist both attitudes. Everyone is unique, and successful jobholders come in many different shapes and sizes.

Another trap is to over-specify the person we are seeking. It is easy to persuade ourself that only a paragon can do what we want. Too many person profiles and job advertisements read like a description of the chief executive. Not only are the chances of finding such a person small; if we were to find them, it is likely that their performance would be poor for lack of scope and challenge, and they would soon leave for greener pastures.

Perhaps the commonest mistake in drawing up person profiles is to use vague, meaningless phrases that can do nothing to help the choice. 'Well motivated', 'good communicator', 'excellent team player', 'enthusiastic and committed' are phrases hardly worth writing. Even if we believe them to be true, no candidate will have much difficulty in demonstrating that they meet the bill.

At the other end of the scale, we can be too precise in drawing up a person profile, inserting criteria which are unjustifiably limiting. Amongst the worst of these are age limits; many people regard ageism as a form of discrimination as wrong as sexism or racism. Arbitrary restrictions based on length of experience are likely to be similarly unjustified; experience is qualitative rather than quantitative. A requirement for specific qualifications can also be unnecessarily limiting; there is frequently a trade-off between qualification and experience.

The good person profile will nevertheless include clear statements. The successful candidate must, for example, be prepared to accept the post for the salary that we offered. They must be prepared to work where and when the job requires. They may need specific skills, such as the competence to operate certain machinery, a current driving licence or efficient shorthand. However, the greater the management element in the post, the harder it will be to define the requirements exactly.

THE ADVERTISEMENT

It is not always necessary to advertise a vacancy. It is common practice to fill the most senior posts through personal contact, often using the services of a search consultant or 'headhunter'. It may be possible to fill the post from speculative applicants or previous lists. However, many medium-sized and large organisations have agreed procedures about the internal advertising of vacancies which are designed to demonstrate to all applicants and existing personnel that justice has been done. Some public bodies are required to advertise vacancies externally.

If we do decide to advertise, the wording of the advertisement can be crucial. Wording which is too loose or inexact, will attract many unsuitable candidates, and much time will be wasted in sifting through them. On the other hand, wording which is too restrictive or uninviting may discourage good candidates. An ideal advertisement will attract a fairly small field (typically between 15 and 30) of highly suitable candidates. To achieve this is not easy, and managers frequently find the help of a professional – either from their own human resources staff or from an external consultant – to be valuable.

If the advertisement is to be placed outside, the job is made harder as most recruiters are aware of the public relations aspect, and are anxious to display their organisation in the best possible light. It is easy to go too far, and paint the picture of a dynamic, young, vibrant team in such rosy colours that the reality, when at last it comes to light, is shattering.

The choice of suitable media is important and requires careful consideration. Both the results and the cost of the choice can vary widely; expert advice is well worth taking.

HANDLING APPLICATIONS

The handling of applications is important. The candidate will judge the organisation by how well their application is dealt with. Above all, getting the right person on board will demand speedy and efficient administration. Good candidates move quickly; if we do not get them, a competitor will. The recruiter cannot afford to lose papers or waste time making a decision.

INTERVIEWING

Selection without an interview is unthinkable, but the interview has been shown to be hardly better than tossing a coin. Many of us like to think that we can 'pick a good one' by instinct, but the research findings are against us. However, its effectiveness can be improved up to a point by the best techniques. There are several elements of effective selection interviewing.

There are many traps. A simple mistake is *to talk too much*. Interviewers need to set the scene, ask searching and relevant questions, and answer those of the candidate. The candidate should do the rest.

A common mistake is *to make a premature judgement*. Inexperienced interviewers judge candidates as they walk into the room, perhaps by the way they walk or shake hands. They then spend the rest of the interview looking for evidence to support their view. Listening can be very selective, and replies which do not fit the view we have formed are literally not heard.

KEYS TO EFFECTIVE SELECTION INTERVIEWING

- Good advance preparation.
- Thorough study of each candidate's papers beforehand.
- Good administration and choice of room, furniture and layout.
- An introductory phase to set the scene and establish rapport.
- Methodical exploration of the relevant aspects of the candidate's cv and aspirations.
- Effective listening.
- Plenty of opportunity for the candidate to ask questions.
- Good note-taking during interview.
- Methodical post-interview assessment.

A related trap is what has been called *the 'halo effect'*. If the interviewer learns of a fact that they regard as strongly favourable (or unfavourable) to the candidate, they will hear only evidence to support that view. The crucial fact may be a high exam mark, for example, a medal for bravery, or involvement in a charity. Sadly, no one achievement can ensure suitability.

Discrimination, or judging a candidate not by what they have to offer as an individual, but by the class or type they belong to, is common. Discrimination by sex or race is illegal. Discrimination by age has already been mentioned. But almost anything can be used to discriminate unfairly. It is difficult to view dispassionately a candidate who went to the same school or college as us, who belongs to the same club or secret society, who has common experience or friends, shared beliefs or a similar use of language.

Effective interviewing is a skill which calls for systematic development, and in which the new manager should ensure he or she is properly trained.

▶ **Checkpoint 6.2**

Are you involved in personnel selection? If so, have you any idea how successful your selections have been? If you have made less than optimum choices, do you know what went wrong? Have you been trained in interviewing techniques?

Performance appraisal

The regular, systematic appraisal of performance is often part of organisational procedure. The objectives may include:

- To check that employees are performing adequately
- To discuss and solve long-standing difficulties
- To help employees' career planning
- To help assess development and training needs
- To document employees' potential for promotion
- To provide a basis for payment by results (while some schemes do all possible to *separate* appraisal from remuneration, in practice this is difficult.)

However, appraisal can be a two-edged weapon. It is very sensitive; good performance appraisal is a powerful tool of management; bad appraisal can do much harm. Appraisal causes tension in both appraiser and appraisee.

Appraisers find it time-consuming. Evaluations difficult to make, interviewing is demanding, especially of those with less-than-standard performance, and promises are easy to make and hard to deliver. Appraisees fear unfair assessments, confrontation and criticism. Many managers are both appraiser and appraisee, and suffer in both roles.

Study the keys to effective appraisal.

KEYS TO SUCCESSFUL APPRAISAL

- Visible commitment from the highest level.
- An open, two-way process.
- Sound, simple paperwork and procedures.
- Explanation to all of why the scheme exists and how it works.
- Training of appraisers and appraisees.
- Effective interviewing.
- Disciplined follow-up of action points.

VISIBLE COMMITMENT FROM THE HIGHEST LEVEL

Appraisal is a management activity that can only work well under a 'do-as-I-do', rather than a 'do-as-I-say' regime. Top management must make, and continue to show, public commitment to all aspects of the scheme. If they are themselves subject to it, better still.

AN OPEN, TWO-WAY PROCESS

Appraisal is an opportunity for both appraisee and appraiser to learn from the past and plan for the future. Systems of confidential reporting offer the opportunity for direct, unfettered comment on performance, personality and potential. However, they are open to suspicions of unfairness, bias and nepotism, and do not offer the opportunity for constructive, two-way exchange. An open system, in which appraisees see all that is written about them and are interviewed by the appraiser, is now accepted as appropriate to the cultures of all but the most bureaucratic and hierarchical of organisations. Most systems now invite the appraisee to contribute, often starting the process by producing their own appraisal of the past year. Virtually all give scope for appraisees to provide their reactions to comments made about them. Most processes offer the right of appeal to a higher authority in case of serious disagreement, although this should be regarded as a sign of failure.

By using an open system, both appraisee and appraiser can learn from the review of the achievements and activities that could have gone better. By concentrating on performance, the unproductive discussion of personality traits is avoided. By allocating at least half the discussion to objective setting, organisational and management support and development needs, a sound basis for the future can be laid.

SOUND, SIMPLE PAPERWORK AND PROCEDURES

Many appraisal schemes have sunk without trace under a weight of paper. Appraisal is at best a time-consuming process for all concerned, and the simpler it is, the better. Records must be kept; there will be objectives and targets, development and training promises and other management action to be monitored. If evaluations are made, they may be needed when promotion is being considered. This year's appraisal may be used as a starting point for next year's.

If the open, two-way approach is used, the documentation is likely to consist of one or two sheets of paper, on which appraisee and appraiser record their comments on the past period and their plans for the next, together with a summary of their discussion. Copies will be needed by each party, and may also be supplied to the human resources function.

A few schemes have rating scales on which appraisers are expected to record value judgements about the appraisee. Some may even refer to personality traits such as honesty or enthusiasm. However, most organisations now see such an approach as counter-productive, leading only to pointless tension and confrontation, and achieving no improvement in performance. Most schemes now use only a few broad headings designed to act as a checklist for both parties; 'achievement of objectives'; 'reasons for non-achievement'; 'next year's objectives'; 'development and training agreed'; 'other management actions' and so on.

EXPLAIN WHY THE SCHEME EXISTS AND HOW IT WORKS

Many organisations provide a simple leaflet describing the purpose of their appraisal scheme and how it works. If we do this, it is best to distribute it annually with the other paperwork rather than to assume everyone has already got, kept and read one. The leaflet will also always need support by face-to-face briefing, and this too should be done before each round of appraisals.

TRAINING OF INTERVIEWERS AND INTERVIEWEES

Poor interviewing is the commonest cause of ineffective appraisal, and training for interviewers is essential. However, it is also very helpful to train appraisees, who frequently fail to get the most out of the scheme for lack of an effective approach to the interview. In practice, many people will be both interviewers and interviewees.

EFFECTIVE INTERVIEWING

Effective interviewing lies at the heart of appraisal. The interview is the chance for both parties to allocate time to talk through achievements, plans and supportive action without interruption and with each other's full attention. It is often best not to hold the interview in the manager's office, if that cannot be private and interruption-free. The office furniture – especially the desk – can also have connotations of status and authority which make a relaxed and productive atmosphere harder to achieve.

> **KEYS TO SUCCESSFUL APPRAISAL INTERVIEWING**
>
> - Prepare carefully.
> - Ensure freedom from interruptions.
> - Use an informal arrangement of furniture.
> - Get the appraisee talking as soon as possible.
> - Establish a flow before tackling any difficult areas.
> - Ask the appraisee for their views rather than stating our own.
> - Invite and take note of feedback on our performance as a manager.
> - Dedicate at least half the time to looking forward.
> - Beware of promises (or implied promises) that cannot be honoured.
> - Set clear, agreed action points by both parties.
> - Finish on an up-beat note.
> - Ensure all actions are monitored and all promises honoured.

The first requirement will always be to establish a relaxed rapport between appraiser and appraisee – both are likely to have some degree of anxiety. How long this takes will depend on the characters of each and their on-going relationship; until this has been achieved, constructive discussion will be impossible. It is often a good idea to get the appraisee talking as soon as possible, preferably in answer to a neutral, non-threatening question such as 'Well, Bill, how has the year gone?' If there is some assignment or aspect of on-going work that is of interest to both, this may form the natural starting point: 'How is the Smith assignment coming along, Bill?'

If there are areas of likely tension, they are usually best left until later in the interview, when both parties have relaxed. The appraisal interview should, in any case, never be used to administer reprimands for failings; these should have been fully dealt with at the appropriate time. It is often best for the appraiser to begin each subject with an open question rather than a statement ('How do you feel the new procedures are working?' or 'What further support can I give you on this?'). To begin with a value judgement ('You have failed badly in getting the new procedures up and running') can only lead to both parties taking up confrontational positions.

About half the interview should be allocated to planning, including the setting of agreed objectives and targets, development and training and agreed management action. Review points for these should be set at appropriate intervals, which will usually be long before the next round of appraisal.

The aim should always be to conclude on a note of positive, forward-looking agreement.

DISCIPLINED FOLLOW-UP OF AGREED ACTION

83

Unless things change for the better, the appraisal has achieved nothing. Appraisee, appraiser and other parts of the organisation such as the human resources function are all likely to have actions to take. One of the quickest ways to bring an appraisal scheme into disrepute is for these actions not to happen.

▶ **Checkpoint 6.3**
Does your organisation have an appraisal scheme? If so, what contribution, in your experience, does it make to management effectiveness? Have you or others experienced problems in the working of the scheme. If so what, and how were they, or how could they be, overcome?

Counselling

Counselling is usually thought of as giving advice. In fact, professional counsellors regard it as a process of facilitation and support, in which they help the subject to structure their own thinking and face concerns positively and constructively, without imposing their own views or solutions.

Because managers are to some extent *in loco parentis* to those who work for them, they are likely to become involved in counselling situations. If you are involved in counselling, there are some keys which can help.

KEYS TO SUCCESSFUL MANAGEMENT COUNSELLING

■ Be alert to unexplained falling off in performance or changes in behaviour.

■ Make informal contact to establish the cause of such changes.

■ If necessary, arrange a private, in-depth interview.

■ If the cause is not work-related, put the individual in touch with specialist help.

■ If the cause is work-related, explore in detail and take corrective action.

■ Monitor results.

84

BE ALERT TO UNEXPLAINED CHANGES

We should be alert to any falling off in hitherto good performance. Indicators may include frequent absence or repeated lateness, signs of heavy drinking, accidents or memory loss, unusual irritability or quarrelsomeness. Basically, any unexplained and continued changes in behaviour or performance are likely to suggest the need for action.

Managers cannot shirk such issues. Humanitarian considerations apart, employees with problems do not work well. They may involve personal problems or aspects of work, whether current issues or longer-term career development problems. Inevitably, managers are in the front line. The difficulty will often centre on how deep and prolonged our involvement should be, and at what stage if any we should bring in other help.

MAKE INFORMAL CONTACT

The early stage of exploring a problem area can be tricky. If the difficulty is obvious as, for example, with a sudden breakdown, accident or drinking episode, it is usually best approached directly. In other circumstances, it may be best to make informal reference to what we have observed, perhaps at a suitable moment in an otherwise standard walkabout. The problem can sometimes be broached during discussion of another, unrelated matter. If the individual does not respond at once, a period of waiting and a second approach may be helpful, unless the symptoms are serious, in which case matters will need to be pressed at once.

ARRANGE A PRIVATE INTERVIEW

Individual privacy must always be respected by discussing problems in private. A well-conducted private interview will also provide the opportunity for a more thorough exploration of the issues, although suggesting it may be felt as a threat. To link the interview with an objective aspect of work ('Can we have a chat to update me with the Smith assignment, Bill?') may help, although it may also appear dishonest. The method of conducting the interview is similar to that of an appraisal interview (see above).

85

Managers are rarely trained in counselling skills or qualified in the many non-work areas that may be involved. Usually, therefore, it is wiser when non-work problems are indicated to put the individual in touch with appropriate sources of professional help at an early stage rather than playing the amateur psychologist. Larger organisations now frequently make provision for professional counselling.

If work issues appear to be central, managers must clearly see matters to a satisfactory conclusion. We must be alert to the possibility that work and private problems may be interrelated. Work difficulties may be caused by underlying personal problems, as, for example when persistent lateness springs from chronic illness in the family, or an increase in error from marital problems. Similarly, personal problems may spring from work causes as, for example, when work stress results in excessive drinking or health problems. Such complex situations may call for expert assistance, in which managers have only an indirect role to play.

TAKE CORRECTIVE ACTION

If the problems are clearly work-based, managers must accept responsibility for their solution. In solving them, we shall need to consider options such as:

- Training (in which the manager may have a direct part to play)
- Changed working practices

- Sharing or reduction of work-load
- Job change or rotation
- Improved equipment or machinery
- Formal disciplinary procedures

MONITORING THE SITUATION

Whatever approach has been taken, it will be essential to monitor the situation for a suitable period to ensure that it has been corrected.

▶ **Checkpoint 6.4**
Have you been involved in a situation in which counselling was necessary to solve a problem in the workplace? If so, how were the difficulties overcome, and with what success?

Individual development and training

The organisation that is able to make good use of the potential of its employees will thrive, but one that does nothing in this way will, in the long term, stagnate.

There are many reasons why managers should develop their people. For some, it is a moral duty. For others, the practical advantages of improved motivation and performance in their present job are adequate justification. For all, the possibilities of so enhancing individual skill that they can contribute to the development of the organisation, either in their current job or in a future one, must be exciting. If we really believe that people are our most important resource, then we must accept that their development is crucial.

Some managers prefer to see development as someone else's job – a matter for the 'personnel department' or the 'training manager'. Such specialists clearly have a role to play. But that role is supportive; the central roles belong inescapably to the individual and his or her manager. Few people, when asked to identify the three or four most important elements in their personal development, will speak of a training course; the majority will refer to a relationship, usually with their boss.

Keys to effective development include:

- Establish a learning climate
- Identify specific development needs
- Decide which development methods can best meet the needs
- Provide the development
- Monitor the results

ESTABLISHING A LEARNING CLIMATE

The term 'learning organisation' is used to describe an environment in which all members are encouraged to develop. Development cannot be confined to the early years of a career; it is no longer possible to gain the skills and knowledge needed for the whole career at or near its start. Techniques, technology, legislation and the needs of society are in a state of continuous change, and all who seek a successful career must keep up to date. The term continuing professional development (CPD) is used to describe this process. Continuing development should become an approach for all staff, in which managers take the lead. We must set an example and give encouragement and practical support. Support may mean day release, flexible working hours, financial support, pay enhancements, and the full use of organisational tools such as appraisal. Many organisations have come to realise that benefits do not come only from training designed to improve immediately-needed working skills. Development should be for the present job, the next one, and even the one after that. Some organisations are convinced that broad, non-work-related education is beneficial.

The words 'management' and 'development' have become too firmly cemented together. It is important not to confine support to those who are seen as high fliers. High fliers do need development for the good of the organisation, but the benefits of encouraging and helping development for all are at least as great.

IDENTIFY DEVELOPMENT NEEDS

An individual's specific development needs in their present post are likely to be demonstrated by less than optimum performance, and may also be picked up by the appraisal process. If changes occur in technology, methods or job content, they are almost certain to give rise to

87

training needs. Development needed for promotion or job change should be established during appraisal. Attendance at assessment centres or longer courses may also be used to establish individual needs for current or future posts.

It may be beneficial to use the services of trainers or consultants to conduct a methodical survey of training needs within an area, especially if major performance deficiencies have been identified or major changes are envisaged.

The process of 'menu picking' from lists of available courses is common, but often does not lead to real benefits.

It is essential to set agreed development objectives in conjunction with the trainee. The more precisely these can be stated, the better, although setting measurable objectives is often virtually impossible. Typical developmental objectives might be:

88

> *To increase X's speed of working by 15 per cent.*

> *To familiarise Q with the new PQR spreadsheet package so that they can use it effectively in their present job.*

> *To reduce rejects produced by Y to fewer than one per week.*

> *To provide Z with the skills and confidence to make an effective oral sales presentation to clients.*

> *To have become familiar with the techniques necessary to introduce a TQM programme across the organisation.*

WHICH DEVELOPMENT METHODS BEST MEET THE NEEDS?

'Training' is often spoken of when 'development' is meant; training is only one approach to the much larger area of personal development. This distinction has considerable practical importance for the manager. To send someone on a course appears to get the problem off the manager's back, but is often the least effective way of meeting a development need. There are many other options.

Each of the methods of development can have a role to play. But probably the strongest development method of all is working closely with an effective, development-oriented manager. Many successful careers owe their success as much as anything to such an influence.

METHODS OF DEVELOPMENT

- On-the-job training
- Special assignments or 'action learning'
- Job rotation
- Programmed or computer-based learning
- Work shadowing
- Attachments or secondment
- Coaching/tutoring/mentoring
- Learning contracts
- Distance learning
- Private reading
- 'Assistant to' positions
- Community roles (e.g. magistrate, club official)

If off-the-job-training seems appropriate, there remain several options:

- Short courses (typically one to three days)
- Longer courses (one week to several months)
- Day release
- Evening study
- In-house courses (possibly on a team basis)

The work of the National Council for Vocational Qualifications (NCVQ) in establishing National Vocational Qualifications (NVQs) for all kinds and levels of occupation is doing much to provide a range of competence-based training and portable qualifications. Managers should know how this impinges on them and those working for them.

PROVIDING DEVELOPMENT

If development is seen as a matter of sending people on courses, it is likely to be subject to budgetary constraints and delays. If other methods are used, the degree of flexibility is much greater, and the chance of undertaking development when it is needed is much higher.

MONITORING THE RESULTS

There is a danger that the purely subjective aspects of course attendance ('How good was the lecturer?', 'Which sessions were of value and which were not?') may be confused with real assessment. If development objectives have been clearly and accurately specified, the monitoring of actual results should be much easier. Even in this case, managers will need a systematic approach. It may be necessary to review results at several points, possibly immediately after the event, and then one and six months later. The act of monitoring will itself help to reinforce the original experience, and may lead to follow-up activities.

▶ **Checkpoint 6.5**
Would you describe your organisation as providing a 'learning environment'?
What development experiences have helped you most in your career so far?
What development have you personally undergone within the last year, and how valuable has it been?

Discipline

Discipline is a dirty word in some views of management today, but without good discipline, management and, indeed, life in society of any kind becomes impossible. Effective leadership and self-management, as discussed in Chapters 2 and 3, will provide the basis for good discipline. There are several additional steps to a complete approach:

- Have as few rules as possible
- Make clear what the rules are and the reason for them
- Have and use a clear, fair disciplinary procedure
- Ensure justice is both done and seen to be done
- Make and keep good records of every case

HAVE AS FEW RULES AS POSSIBLE

Lengthy and complex rule-books have provided the opportunity for the form of 'industrial action' known as 'working to rule'. It is difficult to justify rules so demanding that their observance makes the operation impossible.

MAKE KNOWN THE RULES, AND THE REASONS FOR THEM

Ignorance of the law is no defence. However, as managers, it is essential to draw our organisation's rules to our people's attention. This is usually done when they first join, but will be necessary at intervals later, especially if they move to a new work area with different rules.

Rules are often listed in a handbook given to all, and may be displayed on notice-boards. Unfortunately, people do not always read what they are asked to read – even if, as in some cases, they are asked to sign that they have done so. To make sure, we may have to devote time to a face-to-face run-down when an individual first joins our area, or to a group presentation if any major changes are made.

A CLEAR, FAIR DISCIPLINARY PROCEDURE

Larger organisations invariably have established disciplinary procedures associated with their industrial relations policies. Managers must always be familiar with these; they may need to implement them at a moment's notice, possibly under psychological pressure. A clear procedure can be of great value to any organisation, both for managers and other employees.

91

ENSURING JUSTICE IS DONE AND SEEN TO BE DONE

Any procedure should ensure that justice is done. Managers may need to ensure proper publicity for what happens, as rumours and gossip can distort the record, to the disadvantage of all parties.

KEEPING RECORDS

There will always be a need for full records of every stage of disciplinary action. Even before a formal procedure is started, wise managers will make notes of any events and conversation they have which might have disciplinary implications.

▶ **Checkpoint 6.6**

Have you experienced disciplinary problems as a manager? If so, what did you do about them? Has your organisation a set disciplinary procedure? If so, do you know what it is? Have you ever used it, and if so, did it work effectively?

7

Managing operations

- **Familiar and unfamiliar operations**
- **The elements of operations management**
- **The environment**
- **Machinery and equipment**
- **Materiel**
- **Processes and methods**
- **Control**
- **Problem-solving**

Every manager must be responsible for some kind of output, whether of a product or service.

Familiar and unfamiliar operations

We may be responsible for an area we know well, or one which is completely new to us. Either situation will present both advantages and disadvantages.

If we are managing operations with which we are familiar, we will be well placed to solve problems. We will know what can and cannot be done, the time it should take, and the likely difficulties. Our knowledge and experience will command respect.

On the other hand, if we have been promoted from the area we now manage, familiarity with our old colleagues may worry us. Familiarity with the operation may tempt us to stick to the methods we know and to resist change. Delegation may be difficult. We may prefer to take a job over from a subordinate who has problems rather than help them to find the solution for themselves.

If we know some of the operation at first hand, we may be tempted to spend more time on those aspects, and neglect the others. We may delegate unfamiliar areas or even abdicate from managing them. We may show favouritism to those working the areas we know, and fail to appreciate the work of the others.

If we manage an unfamiliar area we will escape these problems, but will suffer from others. We will have to learn new operations and new terminology; words alone may be a serious difficulty. We will have to ask people to do things we cannot do, and we may not know what is reasonable and what is not. We may spend effort on side issues, perhaps even being deliberately misled. We may have a harder struggle to win the respect of our people.

Whichever situation we are in, therefore, we need managerial skills to succeed.

93

▶ **Checkpoint 7.1**

How skilled are you in the work you manage or expect to manage? What problems do you have, or foresee, as a result? How can these be overcome?

The elements of operations management

Managing an operation of any kind will involve several elements:

- The environment
- Machinery and equipment
- Processes
- Material
- Control

Each of these aspects is relevant to both indirect, office- or knowledge-based operation and shop-floor production.

The environment

After a while, we tend to take our working environment for granted, but it will affect the success of our operation. An unsuitable environment may affect the work directly; temperature, dirt, dust or humidity may affect machinery or the materials used, reduce the efficiency of the process and lower quality. If it is too hot or cold, noisy, badly-lit or unpleasant in other ways, this will affect morale. Workers will be unhappy. Sickness and turn-over rates are likely to be high. An unsafe environment will risk accidents to workers and the work – possibly even to customers or the general public.

Many aspects of the working environment are covered by legislation such as the Health and Safety at Work Act. Managers may have personal responsibility for any infringements, and we will need to know the applicable requirements for our working environment, and to satisfy ourselves that they are being met.

First-line managers often feel that they have little control over the environment of their operation; that it depends on decisions – commonly on the availability of funds – from a higher level. But if we believe that the buck stops here – i.e. with us – we will take a different view. We will look for every feature which is within our control – the arrangement of work stations, furniture or equipment, for example or the way work flows through the area – and ensure that it is the best that we can make it. We will probe control of other aspects, checking the limits of our authority, and who has the authority outside those limits. We will do all we can to influence decision-makers, and be a thorough nuisance if we have to.

94

▶ **Checkpoint 7.2**

Consider the environment in which you work. Does it present problems of any kind? If so, what are they? Who has the authority to put these right? Is there anything you can do?

Machinery and equipment

The development of information technology has made efficient machinery as important in offices as in shop floor areas. Many organisations depend for their success on the quality of their machinery or equipment. Whilst a few organisations do well by screwing the last ounce out of out-dated and out-worn machinery, many more find that investment in the best technology is the gateway to success. It is easy for changes to creep up on us; our machinery may have been state-of-the-art last year, but how does it rate now? We need to keep up-to-date and to know what is available and what the competition is up to.

On the other hand, we must not just change to keep up with Jones plc next door. Many computers, for example, were bought and installed, especially in the 1960s and 1970s, by managers who wanted to keep up-to-date. They had no clear idea of what the equipment could and could not do, let alone of how it could help them meet their operational objectives.

As with the working environment, we may feel that we have insufficient control over the choice of machinery and equipment in our area. But because machinery and equipment often has a more measurable effect on output than the environment, it can be easier to convince others of the need for improvements.

▶ **Checkpoint 7.3**

How familiar are you with the function, operation and safety implications of the machinery in your area? How does it meet your needs? How does it compare with what competitors are using? If it is less than ideal, is there anything you can do about it? Is it properly maintained?

Material

The access to a supply of high quality, unusual or cheap raw material, or to an exclusive supply of components, may be an ingredient in our organisation's success. As with machinery and equipment, we need to keep up-to-date with what is available. An interruption in supplies is something every manager wants to avoid.

MAKE OR BUY?

A key decision for organisations which have the capability to do either will be whether parts and assemblies should be made in-house or bought out. Apart from cost, the decision will involve quality and availability. It may also be felt desirable to maintain links with suppliers – even, in the case of larger organisations, to keep them in business – to help if in-house supplies fail or cannot meet peaks or suddenly increased requirements. Many organisations have developed close links with important suppliers designed to help a long-term relationship which may be crucial to both parties.

Purchasing is an important skill which will, in most larger organisations, be a function in its own right.

STOCK HOLDING

The keeping of stocks is expensive and risky. Not only does it incur financial costs, including interest on the capital and the costs of physical storage, but also the risks of obsolescence, damage or loss. For all these reasons, the lower the stocks the better, always *provided* that they are available when needed. This is one of the dilemmas of production.

For materials brought from outside, the answer to this has been to improve the standards of the distribution industry. In many cases, materials and parts are now delivered within hours or days rather than weeks. The extreme form of this is known as 'kanban' (a Japanese word meaning 'basket') or JIT (just in time). This technique aims, as the name implies, to supply parts at the exact moment when they are required, thus virtually eliminating stock-holding.

JIT can apply equally to materials brought in from outside and part-finished products moving from process to process within the factory. To succeed, it depends on excellent systems, accurate and timely information, and rigid disciplines from all concerned.

CONSUMABLES

Consumables are those supplies which are used during production, but not incorporated in the product; oil, fuel, heat, light and power.

Good housekeeping and careful husbanding of supplies of material and consumables are, of course, always a mark of the effective manager. The twin dangers of over-ordering and over-consumption of consumables can prove expensive. Waste can be too easily taken for granted. However, if it is unavoidable (e.g. swarf, off-cuts and computer paper) it can often prove to be a resource in its own right. It may be suitable for use in other processes for sale, re-cycling or perhaps as fuel.

Many office items (pens, computer consumables and so on) are also particularly vulnerable to petty pilfering. We must keep our eyes open.

► **Checkpoint 7.4**
What consumables and materials does your operation need? Do you know how they are controlled and what they cost? Have you conducted any checks on the efficiency of their ordering, storage and level of use, and if so, with what result? How is waste monitored and what use is made of it?

PROCESSES AND METHODS

The word 'process' is sometimes used in production to mean aspects of manufacture that take place as a result of chemical action (galvanising, etching) as opposed to mechanical aspects such as cutting or assembly. It is also used in the more common way as synonymous with 'method' or 'system'. In whichever sense, the processes or products of an organisation may form one of its principle resources. They may be protected by patents and barriers of commercial secrecy.

Many of the methods used are similar within every organisation; most personnel departments or sheet metal shops, for example, will do things the same way. However, the difference between best and worst practice, even in these common areas, can be surprising. We should grasp any opportunity of finding out how others do things, and be humble enough to learn from it. Public training courses, conferences, the meetings and journals of professional institutions, and our own personal contacts can all help.

The need to update and improve the processes and systems of production often takes second place to meeting current production targets and coping with day-to-day problems. Challenging methods can be unpopular. We are all creatures of habit, and dislike change. It is worthwhile to adopt a systematic approach.

'Method study' is a technique used by both work study (for shop floor operations) and organisation and methods (for others). It aims to check and improve both the effectiveness and the efficiency of systematic work. Method study has four steps.

THE STEPS OF METHOD STUDY
1. Analysis
2. Challenge
3. Creation
4. Implementation

The first three steps depend on pressing probing questions based on what Kipling called his 'six honest serving men': What? When? Which? Where? Who? and, above all, Why? (Why do we do that? Why do we do it there? Why do we it then? Why does he/she do it? Or the 60,000 dollar question – Why do we do it at all?)

Implementation is often the most demanding phase of method study, and will call for much management skill. The people involved will often feel reluctant to accept change, for a range of rational and irrational reasons. There may be a temptation to sweeten change by the introduction of new machinery which is not really justified, or the payment of bonuses, relocation allowances or other financial enhancements. It is for these reasons that method study has been less used than it might have been.

► **Checkpoint 7.6**
Does your area operate any patent or secret processes? Are you satisfied that the processes used in your area are as efficient and effective as they could be?

Control

Control has four elements:

- Standard setting
- Monitoring
- Evaluation
- Correction

It will be seen that these form a sequence, which may be called a 'feedback loop'. This can be applied to any situation involving control. Thus the helmsman of a boat will set a course, monitor his position, evaluate the need for adjustment, and make the necessary changes.

STANDARD SETTING

Production standards must cover three key areas:

- Schedules
- Productivity
- Quality targets

Schedules are a basic requirement for production. We must know what we have to produce by when, whether our operation takes place in the shop floor or the office, and whether our customers are internal or external. Only from this knowledge can we assess our requirements for people, materials and machines. The further ahead we know, the better, although long-term projections will need regular checking.

The ideal situation is steady, unchanging demand. In this happy state we should have few problems. The worst situation is the 'jobbing shop', in which our workload depends on individual, unforeseeable orders. This is the situation in many service operations, such as retailing, health care and transport. In this case, we can only plan on the average of previous demand. We must know that sales of ice-cream last June averaged £1,000 per day; that 50 patients walked into the surgery daily last month; that the 08.30 bus has recently carried an average of 23 passengers per journey.

Such information can often be refined and made more useful. Past demand could be analysed by day of the week and time of day. The ice-cream seller may be able to link sales to temperature, and try to project forward according to the weather forecast. The doctors' practice may take account of the effect of a serious accident or an epidemic. The bus company may take account of the holiday fortnight and the closing of a local factory.

Most organisations do all they can to persuade customers to place firm orders in advance; furniture manufacturers, for example, will usually only manufacture against a firm order; airlines expect the bulk of passengers to book well in advance. Operations in which this does not meet customer expectations (such as the fish-and-chip shop), or where this is physically impossible (such as accident repair shops), can only ask their customers to queue.

The lead-time of what we do will have a big effect. A product such as a new aero engine with a lead time of perhaps 10 years will demand different control techniques from that of a fish-and-chip shop where the owners can fry on demand.

Managers who serve internal customers, such as those responsible for design, training, or recruitment, may find themselves starved of information by their colleagues unless they are prepared to go out and get it.

▶ **Checkpoint 7.6**

How do you know what workload your area must carry, and for how long ahead? If not, how do you plan the use of your resources?

Productivity is crucial to most operations. It is most commonly measured against labour; 'the number of widgets produced per person/hour', but can be applied to machinery; 'widgets per lathe/hour' or other production resources.

Most processes tend to adapt to a standard, rhythmical rate of working. Often, this may be set purely by tradition and practice – even by deliberately restrictive practice. Some operations, such as those on a production line ('the track') may be linked mechanically. The working pace of others is set directly by demand; the telephonist's job is to answer all calls that are made; the complaints clerk has to handle every complaint.

The more complex, varying, creative and responsible the work, the harder control of productivity becomes. In some areas, the number of units may be less important than the quality; it matters less for a designer to produce a particular quantity of designs than that those produced should be of high quality. In work such as selling, productivity can be judged more by success or failure (e.g. in attaining financial targets).

Work measurement techniques (one of the techniques of work study and O&M) are used to establish standard rates of working, against which individuals and whole processes can be measured. Measurement is most often carried out directly by observation and timing, using clipboards and stop-watches. However, in order to minimise the tensions this can cause, pre-measured standard elements may be used. Measurement is easiest in the case of direct, physical work, although measurement in some areas of repetitive indirect work is also practised. Work measurement is most frequently used to set levels of productivity bonuses.

Apart from the human failings of poor management, low morale and inadequate skills, there are three main causes of low productivity:

- Breakdowns and failures
- Mismatch in the system
- Fluctuations in customer demand

Coping with a breakdown without loss of production will call for ingenuity – even inspiration.

Mismatches, such as too many machines and too few operators, are a nuisance. The rate of production may be limited by any element of a process. Most processes have bottlenecks, which hold back the productivity of the other elements. Often, the bottleneck may be temporary – an inexperienced operator, for example, or a faulty machine.

Fluctuations in customer demand may make full utilisation impossible. The worst case is probably demand with high, regular peaks, such as 'rush hour' travel. But we may also be faced with awkward decisions from long-term changes; providing capacity to meet a strong surge in demand can be both expensive and dangerous, and has driven many organisations into bankruptcy.

A regular audit of productivity can bring unexpected opportunities to light. However, this is a sensitive area; both managers and their people may feel defensive about unused resources. We may feel that by declaring unused time, for example, we risk exploitation. We may want to hold resources in reserve against possible surges in demand. We may feel, less justifiably, a reluctance to reduce our empire. The wise manager will resist all these temptations.

▶ **Checkpoint 7.7**

When did you last review the productivity of your operation? What controls the productivity and speed of work in your area? Are you aware of any bottleneck, either temporary or permanent? Are you satisfied with productivity, and if not, what are you doing about it?

Quality standards are vital in any operation. Shop floor production will usually be controlled against standards of quality, which will be fairly straightforward to define. This is rarer in indirect, office-based operations, for which the concept of quality and the way it can be assessed is often harder to define. Whatever approach is adopted, customer satisfaction must be the acid test, whether the customers are external or internal.

▶ **Checkpoint 7.8**

Do you have quality standards for the work of your area? If so, what are they? If not, what should they be?

MONITORING

Production will be monitored against the standards set. Some operations, such as the production of items on which the safety of the user will depend, require full inspection. For most others, appropriate sampling techniques will be used.

In indirect work, monitoring is more likely to involve verbal or written reporting; sales visit reports, for example, or accident reports. Professional work for clients, such as accountancy and consultancy, will require time to be allocated to each assignment.

Traditionally, quality has been monitored by people other than the producers – often by a full-time team of inspectors. However, there have been a number of new approaches in this area. 'Quality circles', in which groups of operators take responsibility for the quality of their production and meet regularly to discuss problems and take corrective action, have become widespread. The philosophy of 'total quality management' (TQM) places the onus for monitoring quality firmly on the producer, at every level in the organisation. This in turn calls for proper training in the techniques involved, and implies a style of management in which responsibility is given to all. TQM has increasingly been adopted as a fundamental organisational philosophy.

For all kinds of work, a delicate balance must be struck between too much and too little reporting. We will need to consider what information we need; we should establish how it can be best obtained; we must ensure we have a system for its capture, storage, access and analysis; and we have to make full and proper use of it. Apart from regular information relating to core activity, we will need to receive, store and send accurate and timely information about unplanned happenings (or non-happenings). Accidents, breakdowns, delays, quality problems and the like will all need to be the subject of appropriate records and communication. Information management is discussed in detail in Chapter 9.

Whatever other elements it includes, monitoring should always involve personal observation by the manager. This does *not* mean, of course, that we should look over workers' shoulders; apart from wasting time, this will upset everyone involved. It *does* mean 'walking the job'; getting round to see how things are and to talk to people at their place of work. Whatever other information is available, there can be no substitute for direct observation.

▶ **Checkpoint 7.9**

Do you regularly get all the information you need to monitor your operation effectively? If not, where are the blockages? How is quality monitored? Have you adopted or considered the use of quality circles or TQM? If so, have they helped? If not, do you think they might help?

EVALUATION

The evaluation of data collected against performance indicators may not always be straightforward. There can be difficulties in using even comparatively simple measures. The hardest is to distinguish between trends and random events. Does a falling-off in productivity or quality call for action, or is it merely a fluctuation that will correct itself? There are statistical techniques to help in this area, and many are now readily available from microcomputer or even calculator programmes. We should know what is available and what can and cannot be done. This subject is discussed in Chapter 9.

If data is qualitative, relying on our own observation, or on other people's oral or written reports, evaluation can be even harder. One danger is to give too much weight to anecdotal evidence; stories about one or two specific incidents which may or may not represent the real situation. Another is to accept inaccurate observation or description of what has happened. Few of us are good witnesses, and the difficulty is worse if there is any possibility of blame or criticism hanging over us.

103

Problem-solving

Evaluation will centre on the identification of problems and the finding of their cause. It is important to distinguish clearly between a problem and a *decision*, as each requires a different mode of thought. Kepner and Tregoe[1] define a *problem* as:

> **A PROBLEM**
> a deviation from a standard for
> which we need to find the cause.

This varies from common usage, and the difference has important practical implications for the manager. If the cause of a deviation is known or we do not need to find it, it is not, within this definition, a problem. If we say, for example:

The quality produced by machine X has fallen off; the main bearing is worn.

---

[1] Charles Kepner and Ben Tregoe, *The New Rational Manager*, John Martin, 1981.

In this case, we do *not* have a problem – we know the cause. We need to make a *decision* about whether, for example, to repair machine X, replace it, or share its work between other machines.

If, on the other hand, we say:

> *The quality produced by machine X has fallen off; we do not know why.*

In this case, we have (assuming we wish to maintain quality) a problem. We must find the cause of the falling off, and only when this is found can we move into the decision-making phase of what to do about it. Decision-making is discussed in Chapter 9.

It is usually dangerous to assume that we know the cause; cause-finding can be a demanding activity, and experience of similar situations can mislead us. Tricky problem-solving can often be done effectively by a group including those directly involved and others, especially those who are good creative thinkers. A rational technique for problem solving is essential.

The definition of a problem given above is based on the existence of a standard; we must know what we expect. There may, for example, be clear reasons for the drop in production quality by machine X, which our production targets should have taken into account. It may, for example, be coming up for routine maintenance. If performance indicators and standards have been set, spotting deviations should usually be straight-forward.

Three stages in problem solving are of special value:

1. It is always helpful, if possible, *to compare situations* in which the standard is being met with similar ones in which it is not being met. Thus the production quality of machines Y and Z may be holding up or even increasing. The cause of the problem must then lie in some-thing distinctive about X when compared with Y and Z.

2. The concept of a deviation also implies a *point of change*; a moment in time at which the standard ceased to be met. Thus the quality from X may have been satisfactory until, for example, a date in early March, when it started to drop away. By identifying the point of change we can narrow the field of search for the cause. What happened towards the end of February or the start of March?

3. Before assuming that we have found the correct cause, we should

always *test our assumption* against all the data, asking whether it fully and completely explains the drop in performance, the distinctions between problem and non-problem areas, and the timing of the change that has occurred. A new operator, for example, may have been put in charge of machine X at the end of February. He or she may not have been properly trained.

Identifying very long-term changes sufficiently early to take effective action is one of the trickiest of all management difficulties. There is no infallible method of doing this. Eternal vigilance is the only hope.

▶ **Checkpoint 7.10**
Do you have quantitative data to assess the success of any aspect of your work? If so, how do you evaluate it? Do you use any statistical processes? What kinds of qualitative evidence do you rely on? How do you assess them? Consider the last serious mistake or problem that occurred in the work of your area. Was the cause known? If not, was a methodical process used to establish the cause, and did it work?

105

CORRECTION

Correction and the processing of rejects is the bane of production. 'Right first time' is a slogan which has helped some organisations, but this will always be a counsel of perfection.

Once in a while, correction may be straightforward; a mistake has been found and is put right. More commonly, we will need to consider whether there have been any indirect consequences. These may include damage to machinery or equipment, personal injury, delay to the schedule, or possibly the loss of a customer's goodwill. The handling of complaints is discussed in Chapter 11.

▶ **Checkpoint 7.11**
How much of the effort of your operation is spent on corrections or the handling of complaints? Might the policy of 'right first time' work, and how much difference would it make?

8

Communication

┌───┐
■ **The elements of communication**
■ **Communicating face-to-face communication**
■ **Meetings**
■ **The telephone**
■ **Written communication**
■ **Communications auditing**
└───┘

Managers sit like a spider at the centre of a web and must communicate in every direction; with those who work for them, their colleagues, their bosses, and their customers. If we fail in communicating, we have little chance of succeeding as managers. This theme crops up many times throughout the book. The purely mechanical aspects of it are discussed in Chapter 9.

▶ **Checkpoint 8.1**
   Do the managers in your organisation communicate well? Upwards,
   downwards, sideways and outside? Do you? If not, what is wrong?

The elements of communication

Every act of communication has six elements:

■ The sender
■ The message
■ The medium
■ The language
■ The receiver
■ The context

If you pick up the telephone on your desk, dial a colleague and say: 'Just pop up to see me, will you, please?':

- You are the *sender*
- *The message* is 'Just pop up to see me, will you?' (but may be more than that – see below)
- *The medium* is the telephone
- *The language* is spoken English
- *The receiver* is your colleague
- *Context* is everything else that might affect the communication

To work properly, all six elements must be right.

THE SENDER

Senders are in the driving seat. They have the message, and choose the medium, the language and the receiver. However, they cannot fully control either the receiver or the context.

THE MESSAGE

Few messages are as simple as they seem. Some writers on communication speak of 'the words' and 'the music'. 'The words' are that part of the message which is open and visible: often actually in the words. In the example above, this is the request for the colleague to visit your office.

'The music' is the hidden part of almost every message. This usually comes from the existing relationship between sender and receiver. In the example, we can only guess what the 'music' might be. If your colleague has displeased you, or made a mistake, the message will convey an unspoken threat. If it is the time of year for merit rises to be announced, it will convey an unspoken message of important news; whether good or bad will depend on their expectations of you. With partners or colleagues who know each other well, the 'music' can be much more important than the words spoken; a single 'Yep' or 'No way' can convey a wealth of meaning.

The danger is that the hidden meaning understood by the receiver may not be what the sender intended. They may take it to be a threat, for example, or as disagreement, boasting or boredom, when we intended nothing of the kind. This is one of the commonest causes of failed communication; it can lie behind quarrels and long-term estrangements between colleagues, friends – even partners.

To minimise this risk, we should try to put ourselves in the place of the receiver, and imagine how they might hear the message. This is discussed again below. We should also clarify our objectives. In management, even simple comments can be misunderstood. Why are we saying it? What do we wish to achieve? What do we wish to avoid? Are there any objectives we would rather keep hidden?

Objectives may be of several types. We may wish to:

- Inform
- Persuade
- Sell
- Impress
- Amuse or entertain
- Obtain action
- Get feedback

If the communication is tricky or important (a major report, a big presentation or a serious reprimand) we should write our objectives down at the start of preparation.

THE MEDIUM

Correct choice of medium is important. The main media of management communication include:

- Face-to-face
- Internal memos
- Meetings and oral presentations
- Letters
- Telephone
- Notice boards
- Newsletters/papers/sheets

In general, face-to-face communication is more effective than using the telephone, and the telephone is usually better than sending a memo. Sadly, notice boards and newsletters are often not very effective. It is a good idea to use more than one medium; to confirm a discussion with a memo, for example; to present a report orally; to back up an important notice with a briefing meeting.

THE LANGUAGE

Spoken and written English are not quite the same language; if we wrote a letter as we would speak to the recipient, it would be long and rambling; if we spoke as we wrote, it would be curt and formal. In written language, grammar and choice of words must be correct. When speaking, small mistakes are less obvious and more acceptable and we can try things in different ways depending on our hearer's reaction.

The other 'languages' which are of great help in management communication are figures and visuals of all kinds. A diagram, picture or graph will often communicate better than any number of words.

The need to use our customer's native language – even if only a halting attempt to convey the courtesy of having tried – is only gradually coming home to native English speakers. There are many crash langauge courses now available for managers.

THE RECEIVER

Many managers fail because they think of communication only in terms of sending; a way of 'telling the troops'. They feel that receiving is automatic and even inferior; that their job is to talk rather than listen. In fact, unless a message is correctly received, it is better not sent. Receiving is as important as sending; listening as important as speaking; reading as important writing.

We must try to get inside the receiver's head, and consider how they will view the communication. We should ask ourself *not* 'what do I want to write/say/argue?', but 'what do I want them to read/hear/understand?' We must write in a way the reader is able to understand; there is no point, when writing for the layperson, in using technical terms, jargon or abbreviations that mean nothing to them. We must set out a case quite differently for someone we believe may disagree with it than for someone we believe is on our side.

For important communications such as oral presentations and reports, we should begin preparation by analysing the receiver – the listener or reader, asking ourselves some questions.

We must also remember that, especially with written communication, we cannot be certain who the receivers will be. Discussions are overheard; letters read by the wrong person. Sensitive and personal issues need special care, and we must remember that industrial espionage does not just happen in books.

RECEIVER ANALYSIS

- Who are we aiming at? How many are there?
- Who (if anyone) do we not want to know?
- Will they be friendly or antagonistic?
- What do they already know about the subject?
- Have they got preconceptions? If so, what?
- Why should they want to listen to us?

---

110   THE CONTEXT

Effective communication will depend on context as much as any other element. The first need will be to try to eliminate interference; other messages, noise, visual distraction or interruptions.

Where communication takes place can make a lot of difference. The same words will communicate differently in our office, our colleague's office, on the shop floor, the street or the loo. Timing is always important, as anyone who has dealings with the media knows. What recent or expected event occupies the receiver's thoughts? A communication last thing on Friday afternoon will not have the same chance as one first thing on Monday morning. If the hearer has a sick child or has just walked out on their partner, any hearing at all is unlikely.

▶ **Checkpoint 8.2**

Consider one or two recent important communications you have sent or received. How effective were they? How might their effectiveness have been improved?

We will now consider the main media of management communication.

Communicating face-to-face

Face-to-face communication is the best way to build working relationships, and as such, essential between every manager and every employee or customer. It is two-way, allowing the sender to assess how the message has been received, and to obtain feedback. It can easily be adjusted to take account of the reaction of the receiver; we can repeat, re-phrase, amend, even withdraw.

The more fraught the communication, the more important that it should be made face-to-face. The manager who seeks to deliver bad news by memo, or through someone else, will rapidly lose credibility.

Face-to-face communication does not take place by words alone. Even more important than the words used are the appearance, tone of voice, facial expression and body-language; studies have shown that together, they contribute almost 90 per cent of the meaning.

The receiving aspect of face-to-face communication – listening – is, as has been said, as important as sending. We must learn the art of active listening.

ACTIVE LISTENING

- Watch as well as listen
- Interrupt as little as possible
- Encourage by nods, smiles
- Don't anticipate or jump ahead
- Don't automatically jump into a silence; wait and see
- Beware of supplying words

Body language is important in face-to-face communication. Unfortunately, it has acquired something of a mystique in recent years; we all both transmit and receive body language naturally. Everyone can interpret the frown of disagreement, the smile of encouragement, the gesture of impatience or anger. However, some people are more alert than others to the smaller signals and better at interpreting them. We should cultivate this sensitivity. If in a conversation the body language contradicts the words, we should believe the body language.

► **Checkpoint 8.3**

Think of someone who you believe is not a good listener. What exactly do they do wrong? How effective a listener do you think you are? Check with friends, colleagues and partners.

Meetings

Frequently, managers need to convey the same message to a number of people. In this situation also, it is generally best to communicate face-to-face. On the other hand, meetings often prove to be a very unsatisfactory method of communication; they can waste time, confuse and demotivate. Ineffective meetings are amongst the commonest sources of complaint amongst managers.

The starting point for an effective meeting must always be to ask 'Do we really need a meeting?' and being prepared to accept the answer 'No'. Regular meetings are the worst offenders. It is always possible to fill up the agenda for a regular meeting, but this may not justify it being held.

Even when called at short notice, a meeting should have an agenda, which should be circulated to all invited. This will help them to prepare, and also to answer the other crucial questions; 'Do I need to be at this meeting? Do I need to be there the whole time?' Each item on the agenda should not merely be a title, but should state the objective – *why* it is there. If there are reports, previous minutes or other working papers, they should be circulated with the agenda, or at worst soon afterwards.

The chair has a clear responsibility for the effectiveness of the meeting.

An increasing number of organisations use some form of meeting, or 'briefing group' on either a regular or *ad hoc* basis. In this way, reactions can be noted, feedback obtained, and personal relationships built up. Such groups work best when the communication flows both ways – when managers pass the reactions upwards, as well as passing messages downwards.

► **Checkpoint 8.4**

How effective are meetings in your organisation? Consider the last meeting you attended. How did it go? What went well and what could have been improved?

EFFECTIVE MEETING CHAIRMANSHIP

- Ensure each item is carefully introduced
- Encourage everyone, especially the shy and newcomers, to contribute
- Avoid dominating the discussion
- Give a fair hearing to all, whatever their views
- Restrain the verbose, self-opinionated and repetitive
- Keep an eye on the clock
- Draw the discussion to a close when it has run its course
- Ensure the decisions and action points are understood and recorded

---

It is very easy for participants to spoil a meeting. There are several rules for effective participation.

113

EFFECTIVE MEETING PARTICIPATION

- Prepare carefully and sufficiently far in advance
- Arrive on time
- Listen carefully to what others are saying
- Address the chair, not other participants
- Never hold breakaway discussions
- Make your contribution as well as possible and then shut up
- Obey the chair
- Restrain personal feelings

THE TELEPHONE

The telephone provides feedback, but cannot (until the video-phone comes into general use) offer the important channels of facial expression and body language. Use of the voice is all-important, and this can also be a problem. Many people lack the skill, or do not realise the need, to use the tone, speed and volume of their voice with special care. There can be attitude problems; some people are afraid of the telephone; others find it brings on incurable verbal diarrhoea.

We can easily be misunderstood on the telephone: everyone has experienced this when trying to communicate with an apparently unhelpful telephonist or secretary. By the same token, it is possible, by skilled use of the voice, to convey a sincerity or friendliness which is artificial, but helps communication more than a brusque or uninterested voice.

The telephone calls for tight disciplines and good administration. Messages taking is a common source of problems. Fiddly as it is, all necessary details, including both date and time of receipt should be noted, together with any message; few things are more annoying than to explain something in great detail to someone, and then to have to do the same a second time because the message was not given properly. Transferring calls can cause difficulties and annoy the caller. Agreed action must be summarised before a call is terminated. Important calls must be logged for future reference.

USING THE TELEPHONE

- Use a warm, friendly voice
- Announce name and department when answering
- Find out the name of the other party at the start, note it down, and use it during the call
- Don't rabbit on; speak up in a clear, friendly way and then shut up
- Only transfer an outside call if it is absolutely essential
- Finish a call neatly, systematically and politely
- Deliver messages promptly and accurately; always write details down

---

▶ **Checkpoint 8.5**
Is there anyone who you fear or hate to have ringing you up? If so, why? What are your faults as a telephone user?

Written communication

Inevitably, much management communication will take place in written form, either as internal memos, letters with those outside the organisation, or reports.

Written communication is often valuable to supplement and support either face-to-face or telephone communication. It is sound practice to follow up an important discussion with a confirming memo or letter.

Few managers enjoy either writing or reading reports. Unfortunately, they are inescapable in many situations, such as to record accidents and other unforeseen events, important meetings, visits and the conclusions of a major assignment.

In all written communication, the aims must be clarity, brevity and accuracy.

Clarity will be better if we have thought about our objectives and then analysed what we know about our reader, as was suggested above. A sound approach to writing is to produce a first draft quickly, and without too much thought; get the mind and fingers moving. If possible, write more than you think you will need; it is easier to cut out later than add. Follow this up with careful editing.

115

EDITING QUESTIONS

- Have I said all that needs saying?

- Have I said too much?

- Is the argument logical?

- Have I repeated myself?

- Are things in the best order? Does the thought flow?

- Have I chosen the best words, and do they mean what I think they mean? (A dictionary or thesaurus helps!)

- What would happen if this fell into the wrong hands?

If we have the time to put our draft away and forget about it – even for a few hours, we will find editing easier. Concentrate on meaning. Do *not* worry about spelling and punctuation at the first stage of editing, but check these at a later run-through.

Brevity will always gain from thinking time; the old saying 'if I'd had more time, I'd have written less' is true. It is almost always possible to improve writing by cutting words – even sentences or paragraphs. Some words and phrases are always candidates for the red pencil: very, actually, really, tend to . . . it is important to note that . . . adverbs (most of which end in -*ly*) are usually (there's one!) unnecessary; adjectives are not much better.

Accuracy should be the subject of a final run through, after we feel the sense is right. We shall look now for spelling, grammar and punctuation. This stage is helped by the spell-checkers now available with most word-processors. Grammatical checking is now possible, although most of us will have to rely for a long time to come on the rule:

> **Keep sentences short and only use words you fully understand.**

Figures always need special scrutiny; nothing gives a critical reader a better opening than a simple mistake in calculation. Layout is worth attention. We should use plenty of space; wide margins, headers and footers. Cramped documents look ugly and are harder to read. For a report, the cover and binding are important; people will always judge a product by its packaging.

It is helpful if we can get someone else to check our writing. Writers always tend to read what they think they have written rather than what is actually on the page.

The machinery of written communication has changed in recent years. An increasing number of managers use their own word-processing facilities. We no longer need to rely on time-consuming dictation or writing in longhand, followed by the delays and uncertainties of awaiting a typescript, corrections and re-corrections. In the past, many managers allowed work to go out that was not exactly as they wanted, simply because they could not confront their secretary with a fourth or fifth set of alterations. With our own word-processor, this need not happen.

The use of electronic mail systems is increasing, allowing instantaneous transmission to any number of points on the network. This too can help effective communication, provided it is not used as a substitute for face-to-face discussion.

The use of fax (facsimile transmission) is steadily growing. As more and more organisations install and learn to use it, the fax has become a substitute for the postal system, enabling business to be transacted in written form in a fraction of the time it once took.

Receiving written communication is also important to most managers. Many feel they have too much to read, and too little time in which to do it. It is possible to improve the speed and accuracy of our reading skills substantially; there are a relatively large number of books and courses designed to do this.

There are many excellent publications and training courses available to help managers communicate better, whether face-to-face, by telephone or in writing.

▶ **Checkpoint 8.6**
Do you have to do much writing? Do you enjoy it? Look at a recent letter or report, and edit it critically. Is reading a problem for you? Have you studied the technique of speed reading?

Communications auditing

A technique known as communications auditing can be used to study the nature and effectiveness of communication within an organisation and suggest how it may be improved. While a full-scale study may be unnecessary or beyond our resources, a careful survey within a defined area can often pinpoint problem areas and suggest solutions. Several books are available that describe the necessary techniques, and some consultants specialise in carrying out major studies.

▶ **Checkpoint 8.7**
Are there major and recurring problems with communication in your area? If so, have they been studied methodically to pinpoint the cause?

Managing information

- **The growing importance of information**
- **Information technology**
- **Gathering information**
- **The storage of information**
- **Processing information**
- **Information retrieval**
- **The communication of information**
- **Using information**

The growing importance of information

Knowledge is power' is a saying that has been around for a long time. However, it is only within the last few years that the importance of information in effective management has been fully realised. Now, Robert Heller's statement that today's manager must be 'superbly informed',[1] commands ever-increasing agreement.

Information has become critically important for two reasons.

Firstly, the pace of change demands a continual flow of information. Some years ago, individuals could absorb much of the information they required for the rest of their working life in a few years of education. This is no longer so; the total amount of knowledge in all areas increases at such speed that everyone faces technological obsolescence.

Change occurs on two main fronts; technology and the marketplace. Effective managers must have the most up-to-date information on both.

Secondly, modern technology makes information readily available. If we are not superbly informed, we can be sure that our competitors are.

[1] Heller, *The Age of Competition*, ASLIB Proceedings, Vol. 40, Nos. 7/8, 1988.

Information technology is not new; but even more than other technologies, IT's rate of development has accelerated almost beyond comprehension in recent years, and continues to do so. Most managers are now computer-literate; in the future, success will go to those who put the ever-growing powers of IT to the best, most imaginative uses.

► **Checkpoint 9.1**

Would you describe yourself as 'superbly informed'? What kinds of information do you need to do your job really effectively?

INFORMATION TECHNOLOGY

Information technology is, and always has been, an indispensable tool of management. The name tells all. IT is the technological help available for information management: any device or machine that can be used for any of the processes listed above. It therefore includes smoke signals, carrier pigeons, tablets of stone, semaphore flags, paper, pen and ink, boxes of cards, filing cabinets, telephones and faxes, filing cabinets, radio and computers.

119

Information technology is sometimes talked about as if it did not exist before computers, but this fallacy can make effective information management more difficult. The management of information is the job of managers in general, and we cannot turn it over to experts. Managers are responsible for defining their information needs. Deciding how they can best be met may call for the help of experts, as in other areas. Cheap, simple solutions may sometimes be more effective than complex, expensive, high-tech approaches; we must not make decisions simply to keep up with the Joncscs.

Information technology in any case embraces several different areas of expertise. Besides computing, the worlds of telecommunications, libraries and office management all play a part. We must mix and match the most relevant and effective contributions from each discipline.

► **Checkpoint 9.2**

What information technology do you use in your job? Would you prefer better technology, and if so, what?

There are six steps of information management.

THE STEPS OF INFORMATION MANAGEMENT	
1. Gathering	4. Retrieval
2. Storage	5. Communication
3. Processing	6. Use

Gathering information

Most managers suffer from information overload. We are continuously deluged with printouts, reports, journals and junk mail from within and without. But despite this flood, we also frequently lack those items which we really need. The first step to effective information management lies in taking control of the information we receive.

WHY SHOULD I GATHER?

'Don't confuse me with facts – my mind's made up' is frighteningly close to the attitude of some managers. We must have information on the performance of our operation to monitor, evaluate and predict its progress. Whatever our function; marketing, sales, production, research and design or human resources, we must also be up-to-date about the relevant technology, the marketplace, the competition, legislation, social and environmental considerations. There may be legal reasons why information must be acquired; taxation, for example, or under health and safety regulations.

On the other hand, we must ensure that we are not suffocated with information that we do not need. Many forms, computer printouts, memos, reports and circulating journals in the average organisation have long outlived their original purpose. Some were not wanted in the first place. We must be prepared to say 'no'.

Rational information-gathering should start by asking challenging questions.

HOW CAN I GATHER?

There are many sources of information. Within our own department, even within our own filing cabinet, there may be exactly what we need. If not, we must make the most of information obtained by other departments within the organisation; there may be someone just down the corridor who has been filing away the information we need for years. Larger organisations often have libraries or information centres, and the skilled people staffing such centres will be only too delighted to help.

RATIONAL INFORMATION GATHERING

We should ask:

- What information do I need to do my job and why?
- What do I intend to do with it?
- Where and how can I obtain this information? From
  (a) internal sources   (b) external sources
- In what form would I prefer to receive the information?
- How often do I need this information to be updated? (a) regularly
  (b) when changes occur (c) when limits are reached (d) never
- What is the value to me of this information? Does it justify the cost?

If we cannot get what we need in-house, we can turn to the many public sources of information, a surprising number of which may prove to be relevant. These include the information services of professional institutions, public libraries, government agencies and the many specialised private information services and consultancies. Much information is now available on electronic databases that can be accessed with a modem and the appropriate software through telephone lines. An increasing amount is available on CD-Rom (the use of a compact disk to hold information in a 'read only' format). If we do not know where to turn, any good reference library will willingly point us in the right direction.

SOURCES OF INFORMATION

- Our own operation and records
- Colleagues and other departments within our organisation
- Our organisation's library or information centre
- Public libraries
- Professional institutions
- Government departments/agencies
- Specialised information services and consultancies

► **Checkpoint 9.3**

Have you ever reviewed your information needs rationally? Do you suffer as a manager from junk mail? If so, can you do anything to stem the flood of useless information? Do you have problems getting information you need? If so, are there resources you have not tried?

The storage of information

It may not be necessary to store information. Much will have served its purpose as soon as we have seen it. On the other hand, everyone knows that if they throw a document away today, their boss will call for it tomorrow. Choosing which information to store and which to throw away can be difficult.

It is also necessary to decide at which point in the information management process to store materials. Unprocessed information is known as 'data'. Much management data is numerical; sales figures, wages costs, daily output volume, number of rejects, staff sickness days, fee income, number of complaints. These may be stored in their raw form. However, to use such data effectively as a tool of management, processing is usually necessary, and it may be more effective to store the processed information. Processing is discussed in the next section.

TO STORE OR NOT TO STORE?

A high proportion of the information most managers receive should be ditched without mercy. There is no value in cluttering up drawers, filing cabinets, microfiches, films or databases with useless history or junk mail. We must be ruthless in using the waste paper basket. On the other hand, what is useless to us might sometimes be exactly what a colleague is seeking desperately.

Information that we believe will have future value, or which we need to compare with or add to information yet to be obtained, must be stored. Effort spent in storing such important information will pay big dividends. Having decided we must store, the next choice will be how best to do it.

We may be uncertain about the need to store certain information. There are two approaches to this problem; to create a method of interim storage, and to weed stored information regularly.

Any storage system should have a 'gate-keeping' process to limit the information that is included in long-term storage. Interim storage is easy to set up in a manual system; the 'pending' tray is the simplest example. While electronic systems can be designed to achieve the same effect, few of them are; their very capacity and ease of use encourages the storage of unnecessary information. This is a trap to avoid, if possible, when setting up the system.

Weeding can be a lengthy process, and requires an understanding of the subject matter which makes it difficult to delegate. Few managers ever get around to it unless, perhaps, they are changing offices or secretaries. If we ever do find the courage and the time, the results, both in terms of emptied filing cabinets and retrieval of long-lost documents can be shattering.

If we have a secretary it is important that he or she knows our views on information storage, and is not industriously undoing all that we have decided.

123

HOW TO STORE

There are many options open for information storage. The choice will involve both common sense and technical knowledge. It is worth making these choices carefully. The methods include:

- Memory
- Files and filing cabinets
- Cards and card indexes
- Pocket books/diaries/organisers
- Electronic databases
- CD-Rom
- Microfilm/fiche

Memory is, for most people, an under-used resource. Managers who can store their most needed information in their heads will always be one up. Memory-improving techniques are sometimes relegated to party tricks, but this is not sensible. There are many ways of improving our memory, and to do so can only improve our effectiveness in the tangled world of day-to-day management.

The vision of a 'paperless office' appears to have receded. Paper seems certain to remain a key tool for the storage of information, and we must not despise it. The traditional filing cabinet or cupboard remains indispensable for storage of correspondence.

E

Many people find a card box or a small thumb-index book the best way to keep telephone numbers and addresses. The ordinary pocket or desk diary still has the edge, for most people, in tracking appointments. The simple pocket-book is in many jobs an invaluable aid; added sophistication, in the form of 'organisers' helps some, although they need sound discipline and can prove more trouble than they are worth.

Electronic aids for the storage of information continue to multiply, from the large mainframe computer down to pocket electronic organisers. Within the office, many managers now have direct access to a PC, and this has at last placed real information-handling power in the hands of the user. An understanding of electronic databases and their use is an essential aid to efficient information storage. The notebook computer, with its massive and readily-accessible memory is establishing its position with those who travel frequently, especially if supported by a modem that gives two-way access to even larger stores of information. The networking of computers widens the availability of stored information, and should, with proper use, minimise the need for duplicate record keeping.

124

There are dangers. The cost of data entry to large databases can be considerable, whether done by filing clerks or keyboard operators. The latest document photographing and scanning techniques may reduce the cost, but run the risk of the storage of massive amounts of unwanted information; junk mail turned into an ever-growing electronic rubbish tip.

If we use mailing lists we shall be very familiar with the problem of matching information and avoiding or removing duplicate records. Electronic information handling has difficulties in this area, as a single difference in a record (different initials, or the absence of a postcode) can prevent a match. Strict entry disciplines and regular, if necessary manual, de-duplication may be the only solutions.

The storage of personal information on computer files is subject to the Data Protection Act, 1986. Managers who store such information or who consider doing this must, therefore, understand their position under this Act, and may need to register. Surprisingly, identical records may be kept manually without restriction.

Microfilm and microfiche have an established position in the field of long-term – archival – storage of large quantities of information such as copy invoices, application forms or whatever. They are, however, expensive and clumsy to use, and not usually efficient for information to which access is needed frequently.

▶ **Checkpoint 9.4**

What methods do you use to store information? Have you reviewed them recently? How good is your memory, and have you done anything to improve it?

Processing information

We may receive information in the form we need it; an internal memo, for example, or a journal article. We may receive it in a form which is suitable for one purpose, but not for another; accident reports, for example, which tell us all we need to know at the time, but which must be summarised into an annual report. We may also, as was mentioned above, get information in the form of raw data; sales or production figures, stock levels and so on. In such cases, processing of some kind will be necessary.

The way we process information will depend partly on how we intend to use the information, but also on how it has been presented to us. There are crucial distinctions between numerical and non-numerical information.

Non-numerical information is harder to process. The art of rapid reading is helpful to managers who must deal with much written material. There are a number of books and courses available to help. Another common need is to summarise or precis a lengthy document. This calls for the skill of getting to the basic meaning of a passage without too much work. A text marker can be a help. Some people find that it helps to jot down a single word or brief phrase to indicate the central idea of each paragraph, and then link these together into meaningful and grammatical prose without the original in front of them. Finally, they re-read the original, to check that the summary contains all the main points correctly.

Most data is presented in numeric form, and is much easier to process, at least by those with a head for figures. Processing will be designed to extract additional meaning, either by statistical manipulation or by setting up comparisons, or to make the data easier to understand, by effective presentation.

STATISTICAL MANIPULATION

It is frequently claimed that there are 'liars, damned liars and statisticians' – at least when no statisticians are within earshot. Whatever truth there might be in this view, it is a fact that statistics can, if properly used and understood, be a considerable help to effective management.

Most managers use simple statistical techniques, such as averaging a set of data, themselves. In doing so, they often become aware that what they have done helps, but not as much as they would like. Large organisations frequently employ statisticians who can help in the most effective processing of data. This is an area in which a little knowledge can be dangerous, and for large or important applications we may need professional help.

RATIOS

126

Ratios compare one set of data with another in a standard form; 'so much of A per unit of B'. They are often used as an aid to financial control, and are referred again in Chapter 10. There are many other situations in which ratios can help management by showing a situation more clearly than the raw data; rejects per 1,000 units produced; days sickness per days rostered; complaints per units sold. The results can often be graphed to enhance understanding even further.

STATISTICAL PRESENTATION

To aid understanding, data is often plotted in graphical form. There are five simple, common and valuable forms of graph: line graph, histogram, pie chart, cumulative frequency curve and scatter diagram.

In the simple *line graph*, one set of data is plotted against another to which it is continuously related, using a two-dimensional grid, and a line joins each successive point in the plot (see Figure 9.1).

The line graph is ideal for applications in which we want to track the changes of one set of figures against another. The most common occurs when we want to watch changes over time. An important management application of the line graph is the *control chart*, in which lines are drawn in advance on the graph to indicate a band within which no action is necessary. If a value falls outside the band, then the need for control action is indicated (see Figure 9.2).

Fig. 9.1   A line graph

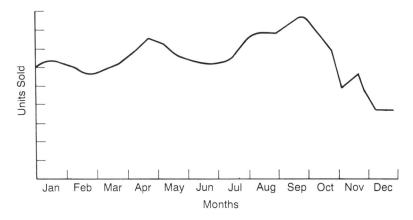

Fig. 9.2   A control chart

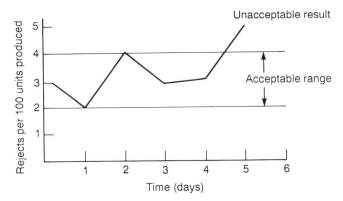

Fig. 9.3   A vertical histogram

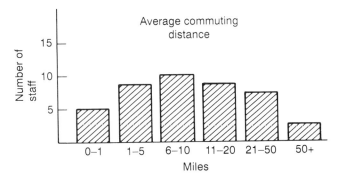

The histogram (Figure 9.3) is the best form of presentation when one set of data is recorded in a series of equal batches; e.g. monthly totals. It is essential to use a histogram when representing a set of data in which the items are not directly related to one another, such as sales totals by region. A horizontal histogram works best if results are distributed about a central point (Figure 9.4).

Fig. 9.4 A horizontal histrogram

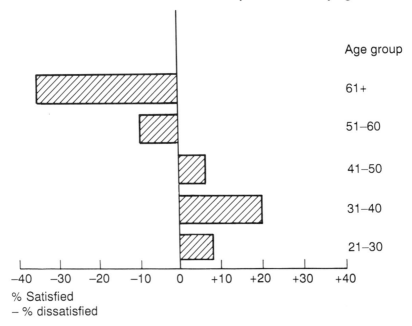

% Satisfaction with the Government's performance by age

The *pie chart* uses the segments of a circle to represent the proportions into which a whole is divided (see Figure 9.5).

The pie chart is most useful when our aim is to compare proportions within a finite total; e.g. the sales income from different products during the previous month. It is often an alternative to the histogram.

The *cumulative frequency curve* uses a two-dimensional grid like the line graph, but one set of data is added (or 'cumulated') from one end of the plot to the other. It can be useful to show how changes occur over a set period of time, such as a week or a year (see Figure 9.6).

Fig. 9.5 A pie chart

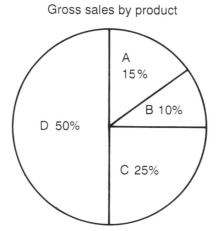

Gross sales by product

Fig. 9.6 A cumulative frequency curve

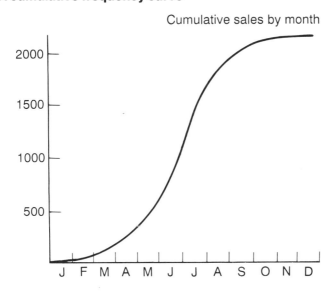

Cumulative sales by month

The *scatter diagram* plots data about single events in two dimensions, using a dot or a cross to place each event. It is helpful when the correlation between two aspects of a set of events is not perfect (see Figure 9.7).

Many desktop publishing and other software packages can now present sets of data in a variety of graphic forms at the touch of a button.

► **Checkpoint 9.5**

Do you receive data or information which needs processing? If so, how do you process it, and are you confident your methods get the best from the data? If not, can you think of any better approaches to processing it?

Fig. 9.7 A scatter diagram

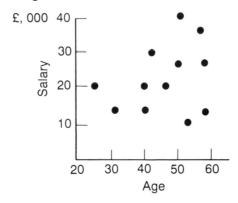

Information retrieval

Otherwise admirable managers often waste an appreciable proportion of their time trying to retrieve information. Whether it is seeking a telephone number, letter or report, or sorting through piles of printouts for the vital indicators of a malfunction, this apparently simple need can waste endless time, raise tempers to flashpoint, and may possibly result in an ill-informed decision.

If information has been efficiently stored, retrieval should, in theory, be efficient; well-filed letters can usually be located when needed. More commonly, problems arise when it is desired (or unavoidable) to access information by an unexpected criterion, or by a combination of factors. We can usually find a telephone number by the name of an organisation, for example, but may have problems locating it by the name of the person within it that we last spoke to. There may be no difficulty in listing all the customers who have bought our product X within the last month, but it may cause much work to establish which of these were new customers and which were regular customers.

It is in this area of information retrieval that information technology shows its greatest advantages. Not many of today's managers may have sought to retrieve information by inserting a needle into a pack of cards, but before the ready availability of computing power, edge- or centre-punched cards formed almost the only method of sorting data by multiple criteria. Modern database packages offer the facility of searching data by almost any criterion or combination of criteria, thus providing an immensely powerful management tool.

Electronic database storage can be of value in virtually any function. In personnel, for example, it can help to find candidates with specific combinations of experience and qualifications required by a vacancy. In sales, it can identify customers with a particular profile as sales targets for a new product. In marketing, it can analyse the characteristics of competitive products and their markets. In production, it can isolate the features of those machines or processes that are prone to failure.

▶ **Checkpoint 9.5**

Do you have problems accessing information? If so why, and what can you do about it? Do you use a database? If not, might it help?

The communication of information

Wide and effective communication is one of the keys to management effectiveness. The importance of the inter-personal aspects of communication, whether face-to-face, by telephone or in writing, were discussed in Chapter 8. It is worth looking briefly now at the mechanical aspects of communication.

Few technologies have changed faster in recent years than communication, and change continues at a bewildering rate. Indeed, one of the principle problems facing managers is the timing of investment in new technology. If we do it too soon, we risk being saddled with undeveloped and unreliable equipment, and we will sacrifice large amounts of useful life from our old equipment. If we do it too late, we risk losing the advantages of being at the front of the field.

THE TELEPHONE

The telephone is already 100 years old, and after many years with little change, it has now moved into a period of important development. The mobile phone and the answering machine both offer help to managers, as do many of the detailed features of a modern telephone system.

The *mobile phone*, whether in car or briefcase, has come in for a good deal of flak, even from the Chancellor of the Exchequer. Many see it as little more than a status symbol and a nuisance in public places. In fact, it can offer real advantages to managers, especially those who travel far and frequently. We must be prepared, if necessary, to put up with occasional ridicule in order to make use of what, for some, is a valuable new tool.

More managers are finding the value of a *telephone answering machine* in their office. Such machines are now so cheap that even the tightest of budgets can usually afford them. However, good discipline is essential, and those who leave messages must be confident that they will receive an answer.

Modern telephone systems offer many useful features, such as automatic transfer of calls when an extension is engaged or when there is no reply. We should make sure we know what our system can do, and make full use of it.

Tele-conferencing, or the use of a combined audio and video link via telephone lines has been the subject of experiments by some organisations. It requires expensive, specialist facilities, and is felt by some to have limited practical advantages as a mode of communication. Its value in day-to-day management seems likely to be small, but it may be advantageous for some international operations.

COMPUTER NETWORKS

The connecting of individual micros or work-stations into networks, allowing the exchange or use of common information, is now rapidly spreading. It is already possible to transmit information over telephone lines by computer, modem and communications software, thus extending the use of networks globally.

Electronic mail systems are becoming commoner within large offices. They offer the advantages of virtually instantaneous transmission of the written word to a number of destinations, together with storage and the ability to produce hard copy. However, they are rarely of sufficient value by themselves to justify the establishment of a network in the absence of other factors.

FACSIMILE TRANSMISSION

Facsimile transmission of documents has now become so common and cheap that it seems likely to replace postal services for much normal correspondence. It has already replaced telex, except for overseas applications.

VIDEO AND CLOSED-CIRCUIT TELEVISION

Video and closed-circuit television (cctv) help some managers with specialised needs such as the control of processes and operations, and in security applications. A few large organisations use video as a means of communication from the top level downwards, but with limited success.

▶ **Checkpoint 9.6**
What methods do you use for transmitting information, externally and internally? Could they be improved, and if so, how?

Using information

After all the work, information management is a waste of time unless the information is used to good effect. It has been traditional in many larger organisations to collect and store much information that is not properly used – this is one of the curses of bureaucracy. This happens for one or more of several typical reasons:

- The boss once asked for it
- The boss might ask for it
- It might come in useful
- We've always collected it
- We didn't know you collected it as well
- No-one's ever challenged us about it

Effective managers must, therefore, regularly challenge their own information management by asking themselves questions about information they hold.

Three of the most important and typical management uses for information are for problem-solving, decision-making and forecasting. Problem-solving has already been discussed in Chapter 7.

> ## CHECKS ON THE VALUE OF INFORMATION
>
> - What, exactly, is that information used for?
> - When was that kind of information last used, and why?
> - What are the costs and benefits of having that information?
> - What would be the consequences of not having that information?
> - Can that information be collected, stored, processed or communicated more efficiently?
> - Can we share that information with others?
> - Can we share information held by others?
> - Are there additional uses to which that information could be put?

DECISION-MAKING

Managers must be decision-makers. In modern, democratic management cultures and also in bureaucratic organisations, this role may be less clear-cut, but the manager's involvement can never be eliminated. Decision-making is an essential aspect of the management task, and can be needed in any part of the management sequence.

Some believe that the strong manager will never change a decision he has made. Clearly frequent changes, or changes which originate from uncertainty or fear, can be very damaging. However, it will always be wiser, if the evidence indicates that we have made a mistaken decision, to reverse it rather than soldier on into worse trouble.

Kepner and Tregoe[1] define a decision simply as:

> **A DECISION**
> **'A choice between alternatives.'**

This implies that, as discussed in Chapter 7, the cause of any problems has been found, and the manager is at the point of choosing a course of action to follow.

A methodical process for multiple choice decision-making is of great help

---

[1] Charles Kepner and Ben Tregoe, *The New Rational Manager*, John Martin, 1981.

in identifying what facts are essential, and properly using those facts that we have. Here is such a process:

STAGE 1

Rational decision-making begins with a clear statement of the decision being made. It is always best to write the statement on paper; this helps us to clarify our thinking and provides a record for future reference. If more than one person is involved, a written statement is essential. Decisions often imply other decisions already made. Thus I might write:

I am deciding which house I shall buy.

This implies that I have already decided we are buying a house rather than a flat, and that I am buying rather than renting.

STAGE 2

The second stage is to list the objectives we wish to achieve from the decision, and the resources we can use in achieving it. For the house, I might write:

- Must cost no more than £100,000
- As near to work as possible
- Must have at least three bedrooms
- Southerly aspect for the main rooms
- Double garage
- Good decorative order

STAGE 3

We can then split the objectives into Musts – factors we are not prepared or able to compromise on – and Wants – those we want as much (or as little) of as possible. We can then weight the Wants to indicate how important they are to us. The rewritten list might be:

Must
- Cost less than £100,000
- Have at least three bedrooms

Want	*Weight*
■ Southerly aspect for the main rooms	10
■ As near work as possible	8
■ Double garage	8
■ Good decorative order	5

STAGE 4

It is important that our list of objectives should be produced and refined *before* we start looking for alternatives – in this case, estate agents, details and houses with 'for sale' boards. In this way, we shall:

(a) be less influenced by sales talk.
(b) be able to concentrate on the information we need.

We now seek information about possible alternatives. If a house fails a Must objective (e.g. costs more than £100,000, or has fewer than three bedrooms) we can reject it without needing any additional information. For the rest, we will obtain and record information about each against each Want objective: how near it is to work, what the aspect is of the main rooms, the decorative order and whether there is a garage, and if so what size.

136

STAGE 5

This stage involves comparing each alternative against each Want objective, giving it a score, multiplying each score by the appropriate weights, and totalling the result for each alternative (see Table 9.1).

Table 9.1 Choice of House

	Wt	Sc	House A		House B		House C	
			Sc	W*S	Sc	W*S	Sc	W*S
Aspect	10	5	50	10	100	8	80	
Dist. to work	8	10	80	9	72	3	24	
Double garage	8	6	48	6	48	10	80	
Dec. order	5	3	15	8	40	10	50	
Totals			193		260		234	

STAGE 6

At this stage we must make the decision, based on the scores. We will look at the differences; if they are reasonably large, we will accept the result. In this example, House A should be rejected. But we must be reasonable; if several results are close, a small change of weight or score might reverse the order. In this situation, we must check our facts and obtain more accurate information before deciding. In this example, it would be sensible to do this to confirm that House B should be our choice.

By using a rational process of this kind, we know what information we need, what is irrelevant, and can devote our effort to the former.

▶ **Checkpoint 9.7**
Consider an important decision with which you have recently been involved, in business or private life. Was a rational process used? Does the decision still appear sound, or is there now a fear that it could have been better made?

FORECASTING

It is the dream of every manager, as of many human beings, to have a crystal ball with which they can foretell the future. There is no such tool, as wise managers must continually remind themselves. More operations have got into difficulty by basing their decisions on over-confidence (or blind ignorance) about the future than in any other way.

137

However, we cannot plan without making assumptions about the future, and some kind of forecasting is therefore unavoidable. The two basic approaches to forecasting (disregarding the I-Ching and crystal balls) are experience-based judgement and statistical data.

JUDGEMENTAL FORECASTING

In judgemental forecasting, those with a good knowledge of the subject are asked to give their considered judgement. We must always formulate the most precise question (or questions) possible; if we ask vague or ambiguous questions we shall get even vaguer and more ambiguous answers, as those who approached the oracle at Delphi used to find out to their cost.

Any relevant available data or background information should be provided to those we approach, but in completely neutral terms; it is essential that the views of the enquirer should not bias those being asked. This is particularly important if the enquirer is a senior member of the organisation; nothing is gained by mere endorsement of the boss's views.

The consultation can take one of three forms; it can be done in a meeting, by single written enquiry or by stepwise enquiries. A meeting offers the opportunity for views to be exchanged and developed, but there is a danger that strong personalities, those with clearly-formed views or political objectives may unduly influence the rest. The single written enquiry can be simple to process, but offers no feedback mechanism. The stepwise process (sometimes known as the Delphi technique) feeds back the answers given to the first enquiry to all panel members, who are invited to use them to modify their views if (and only if) they wish to do so. This step can be repeated a second or even a third time if desired. It is also possible to call a meeting of the panel after they have committed themselves to a first answer.

STATISTICAL METHODS

Statistical forecasting techniques require good specialist knowledge, and managers who without such knowledge should be cautious in this area. It is useful, however, to be aware of the main approaches and their strengths and limitations.

138

The analysis of time series (e.g. weekly sales over a year) can help forecasting by picking out seasonal variations and random events, leaving the overall trend more clearly visible. Thus, for example, if we are looking at a set of weekly sales figures, we will immediately realise that merely to look at individual values will show little. There may be random effects, without any significant cause. There may be seasonal changes. There may be peaks and troughs related to special occasions such as a bank holiday or a period of particularly hot weather. A simple average over the last 12 months gives as much importance to what happened 12 months ago as to the figures for last week, and will not help much; if there has been a trend during this period, the average will do nothing to show it.

By using a smoothing technique such as a moving average, random effects will be reduced, but other significant changes may be masked. Only by using the help of fairly sophisticated statistical treatment can we feel confidence that we are getting the clearest message from the data. The same is true of data about rejects, breakdowns and almost any measures of a continuous process or series of events. Exponential smoothing is a technique that gives the highest weighting to the most recent value, and is therefore likely to be better than a simple moving average. There are a number of much more sophisticated techniques, of which the best known is the 'Box/Jenkins' technique. However, forecasting based on one variable only – as in 'univariate' methods – is often less satisfactory than others, tempting as it may appear.

'Multivariate' techniques relate time series of more than one variable; weekly sales and telephone enquiries, for example. They are usually most successful if one or more 'leading indicators' can be found. These are series whose changes are found to precede changes in the series of most interest. Thus average daily temperature between Tuesday and Thursday might be found to be a leading indicator of ice-cream sales on Saturday, or number of building starts may act as a leading indicator of retail sales six months later.

CHECKING OUR ASSUMPTIONS

Whether we need to use a systematic study or not, we must make some assumptions about the future. The keys to success in this trickiest of areas include:

- Reviewing our assumptions about the future regularly
- Assuming that things will continue with little change unless causes of change can be clearly identified
- Collecting the widest range of the most accurate information available
- Using the best statistical treatment of the information, but only as one piece of evidence
- Getting the widest spread of informed opinions and advice
- Trusting neither our own or others' opinions exclusively
- Making a final judgement according to our own wisdom

139

▶ **Checkpoint 9.8**
Do you use information for problem-solving, decision-making, forecasting or any other management process in a systematic way? Are you satisfied with your use of information? If not, how would you like to improve it?

10

Managing finance

> ■ **The function of accountancy**
> ■ **Financial accountancy**
> ■ **Management accountancy**

140

Words are not enough for effective management communication; to be fully effective, managers also need to get information from figures, and convey information to others in the same way. Unfortunately many people are not happy dealing with figures. The advent of pocket calculators and computers has helped, but the problem still looms large for many. Managing finance can be a potent source of anxiety.

The function of accountancy

Theoretically, accountants are there to help. Their job is to assess, record and communicate the financial implications of management action. There are two approaches: financial accountancy, and management accountancy. The simplest way of defining the difference between the two is that the financial accountant's main task is to satisfy those outside the organisation, while the management accountant seeks to serve those within, and especially – as their title implies – the managers. In larger organisations, these may be the responsibility of a separate person or department. Smaller organisations may employ only a financial accountant or buy in all the accountancy services that they need; in such organisations, managers must be their own management accountants.

Accountants also draw a distinction between accountancy and book-keeping, They see the latter as the day-to-day work of recording financial information, usually carried out by unqualified or part-qualified staff. The evaluation and final presentation of such information is seen as the job of qualified accountants. Crucial amongst book-keeping tasks is ensuring that wages and salaries are correctly calculated and paid.

▶ **Checkpoint 10.1**

What accountancy services does your organisation employ? Do all or any of them supply a service directly to you? Do they help you to manage?

Financial accountancy

Accountancy methods and terms have changed only slowly, but their role in ensuring financial probity for the benefit of owners, employees and the state justifies what some see as a conservative approach. Most managers, especially in larger organisations, do not need an in-depth knowledge of financial accountancy. However, especially if they are also owners or partners, they will need an understanding of basic concepts and the terms used to describe them. The aim of this section is to provide that. Those who need more will be able to obtain help from books and courses specially designed for non-financial managers who require an understanding of finance.

141

THE ROLE OF FINANCIAL ACCOUNTANCY

The role of financial accountancy is to produce records for the organisation in a standard form that meets legal requirements. Such accurate, standard records are needed for two essential reasons: to protect the owners of the business and the revenue of the state.

The records must give the owners of the business information about their property. The ownership of organisations can be one of six main kinds:

- Sole trader
- Partnership
- Private limited company
- Public limited company
- Company limited by guarantee
- Public ownership

Sole traders have, as the name implies, sole ownership of a business. Some smaller organisations are owned by two or more *partners*, under agreements that define how financial responsibility and returns will be shared. Both sole traders and business partners are personally liable for any debts that their business incurs.

Limited companies are those in which individuals or other organisations own shares. They are 'incorporated', which means they have a legal existence which is separate from any individual owner, and they can sue or be sued as a body. The financial liability of shareholders is limited to the face value of their shares. In times of profit, shareholders receive dividends.

Public limited companies must have a share capital of at least £50,000. Such companies are designated by the abbreviation 'plc'. The price of their shares is regularly published, and they can be bought and sold publicly by anyone.

142

Private limited companies, which are designated 'Ltd', have shares which can only be bought and sold in private transactions.

Some charitable organisations, institutes and similar bodies may be *'companies limited by guarantee'*; such bodies do not make profits or declare dividends.

Organisations may be *owned publicly* by local or national government or other public bodies. For them, account must be rendered to the local council, to Parliament, or to a specially appointed authority.

In every case, the law lays down the financial records that must be kept, and the procedures for their publication or presentation to interested parties.

Financial accountants also have a key role in keeping the records necessary for tax purposes. The main taxes are:

- PAYE (pay as you earn) on the remuneration of employees
- NI (national insurance) on the remuneration of employees, split between employer and employee
- VAT (value added tax) on most purchases and sales
- Corporation tax on business profits

The need to deal with ever more demanding tax authorities and to handle ever more complex tax legislation is one of the principle roles of financial accountancy.

AUDITING

The law lays down requirements for the auditing of financial records. Auditing is a detailed and independent check of all financial records and the documents or other data on which they are based. This is also the task of financial accountants who must, in this case, be employed by an independent firm.

Auditors have legal power to examine all relevant documents, and to ask questions of anyone involved. Most managers will know what 'having the auditors in' means.

Some large organisations have their own internal auditors, who will make similar checks to ensure that all financial documentation is in order, but will not have the power to carry out the auditing required for legal purposes.

143

THE BASIC ACCOUNTING CONCEPTS

As has been said, managers do not normally need more than a basic understanding of financial accounting. The remainder of this section aims to explain a few of the commonest concepts that managers are most likely to encounter or become confused over. For the rest, no manager should hesitate to challenge their accountant colleagues to explain their meaning in simple English.

The concepts and terms to be covered here are:

- Trading and profit and loss accounts
- The balance sheet
- Depreciation
- Cashflow
- Management ratios

TRADING AND PROFIT AND LOSS ACCOUNTS

The financial accounts of every kind of business are put together at intervals (often once a month, but some organisations use four-weekly accounting periods) to provide a picture of how things are going. The first summary (after various checks and additions) is called the *trading account.* This records the value of all sales (*turnover*) and any other sources of income. It also records all expenditure which can be directly related to sales, such as raw materials and consumables. The difference between the two is called the *gross profit* (or *loss*).

Fig. 10.1 Trading account

XYZ LTD

TRADING ACCOUNT, JULY 1992

	£	£
Sales of goods	10,000	
Total income		10,000
Material purchased	2,000	
Consumables	125	
Cost of sales		2,125
Gross profit		7,875

Costs which are not directly related to sales (rent, rates) are called *overheads*. In the *profit and loss account* these are totalled, and subtracted from the gross profit to produce the *net profit* (or *loss*).

Fig. 10.2 Profit and loss account

XYZ LTD
PROFIT AND LOSS ACCOUNT, JULY 1992

	£	£
Gross profit		7,875
Rates	1,000	
Rent	1,850	
Electricity	600	
Telephone	320	
	3,770	
Net profit		4,105

Accounts are totalled for each period of twelve months –the *trading year*, or the *financial year* to produce annual accounts. The financial year is not necessarily the same as either the calendar year or the tax year (which runs from 6 April one year to 5 April the next).

THE BALANCE SHEET

The *balance sheet* is a set of figures summarising the financial position of an organisation any given point in time; usually at the end of the financial year. The items it records are *capital* items, as opposed to the items listed on the profit and loss account, which are *revenue* items.

Capital items are those which retain a value over a period of time; a building, or a long-term loan. Revenue items refer to an event taking place at a specific moment; a sale or purchase. This distinction is of great importance in management. Revenue expenditure (e.g. telephone or fuel bills, wages costs) has no future value. Capital expenditure (e.g. purchase of a computer or a van), on the other hand, creates a value that remains over a long period of time. The value of capital items may increase (e.g. the value of a building or a work of art), although in most cases it will decrease, or *depreciate* over time (e.g. the value of a car or a machine). Because of this, expenditure on capital items is not included in the profit and loss account, or deducted from the profit.

145

The balance sheet has two main sections; the first shows the *assets* of the organisation – basically what it owns. The second shows how this has been financed; where the money for these assets has come from.

The assets section is split into three sub-sections; *fixed assets*, *current assets* and *current liabilities*.

In the *fixed assets* section are listed the current values of all capital assets that are expected to retain their worth over a long period; buildings, land, machinery and equipment, fixtures and fittings. It will also usually include amounts for at least two intangible assets; the value of the *goodwill* or trading reputation of the organisation, and a capital value for any leases held.

In the *current assets* section are listed the current value of assets that may disappear in a comparatively short time; stock-in-trade and amounts owing (to *debtors*).

The *current liabilities* section lists the debts currently owed by the organisation (to *creditors*). The difference between the current assets and current liabilities is known as the *working capital*; it is essential for financial health that this should remain positive.

The *financed by* section will list the sources of the organisation's funds; the value of shares issued, long-term and loans and the amount of profit (or loss) carried from the profit and loss account in both the current and previous years.

The totals of the assets and financed by sections must be the same – the 'balance' of the balance sheet. Figure 10.3 shows an example balance sheet.

Fig. 10.3 Balance sheet

XYZ LTD
BALANCE SHEET AT 31 JULY 1992

	£	£
Fixed assets		
Goodwill	10,000	
Lease	2,000	
Machinery & equipment	5,000	
Van	3,500	
		20,500
Current assets		
Debtors	1,234	
Stock	3,500	
Bank	2,550	
	7,284	
Current liabilities		
Creditors	2,100	
Net current assets		5,184
('working capital')		
Financed by		
Capital, Partner A	10,000	
Capital, Partner B	10,000	
Retained profit	5,684	
		25,684

DEPRECIATION

The value of most fixed assets (cars, machinery) goes down as time goes on and they become worn out and obsolete. *Depreciation* is the method of reflecting this loss of value in the accounts. There are several methods of doing this, but whichever is adopted, the overall effect is the same; an amount is subtracted from the value of the asset as shown in the balance sheet, and added to the total of overhead costs in the profit and loss account.

Depreciation is not 'real money', but only a means of recording the fact that assets lose value. It must not be confused with a *sinking fund*, which is created by the putting aside of amounts of real money so that they will be available for the purchase of new equipment when needed.

CASHFLOW

The ability to pay debts when they fall due is fundamental to the financial health of a business. It is of little help to have equipment worth £5 million, or a contract that will produce make a profit of 10 million in two years' time, if we cannot pay this week's wages bill.

Financial difficulties culminating in bankruptcy may be caused by an inability to pay debts when they become due. Creditors (often banks which have lent the organisation money) will sometimes allow extra time to pay if they believe the organisation is fundamentally sound. It may be possible to repay debts by borrowing from a different source ('re-financing'). But sooner or later, an inability to meet financial obligations will catch up on us. Maintaining a healthy cashflow must always, therefore, be a key task of the financial accountant.

MANAGEMENT RATIOS

Ratios, or a comparison between two values, can be a useful tool for management control. They can be used to compare the performance of different units – the various subsidiary companies in the group, for example, or all the shops it owns – or the same unit at different points in time. There are a number of ratios relating profit to other variables: net profit/total assets; gross profit/capital invested; net profit/sales. Ratios involving current assets include: current assets/current liabilities and – what is known as the 'acid test' ratio of solvency – current assets less closing stock/current liabilities. The many possible ratios involving sales include: sales/total assets; sales/stock; sales/debtors.

▶ **Checkpoint 10.2**

Do you see your organisation's accounts? Are you able to interpret a balance sheet? Do you use any accounting ratios to help you manage? Do you feel a need for more knowledge of financial accountancy than you possess? If so, why, and what are you doing about it?

Management accountancy

Management accountancy, as may be guessed from the name, seeks to give managers the information necessary for proper control of the financial aspects of their operation.

Until recently, many managers did not have such control. Even today, the level at which financial control over various aspects is exercised within an organisation varies. Clearly authority for the largest items of capital expenditure (building a new plant, or buying a new office block, for example) must be reserved to the highest level. Major financial decisions usually require the authority of the top decision-making body – the board, council or whatever – and may not be delegated to managers at all. However, below this level there has been a continuous move over recent years, particularly within the private sector, to delegate financial control as far down the organisation structure as possible.

The reason for this change is two-fold. Financial control of one's operation is for most managers a motivator; it increases their sense of commitment. It also helps directly to improve performance, because it is a key area in which authority and responsibility must be matched as closely as possible. If we are responsible for making a product, we will be better able to do so if we also have the authority to buy the tools we need.

Such delegation is usually confined within specific limits. Managers may, for example, be authorised to spend up to £100,000 on capital equipment, to make repairs costing no more than £1,000 each, or to recruit employees up to a certain grade or number. Two techniques go further than this; the concepts of cost and profit centres.

COST AND PROFIT CENTRES

Many organisations have created *cost* or *profit centres*. These are units within the whole organisation under the control of a manager who has been delegated authority for control of costs (in a cost centre) or both costs and revenue (in a profit centre). If a company takes over another, it will often decide to run it as a profit centre. Geographically separate sites, distinct product or service lines and departments or functions may be controlled in this way.

148

An increasing number of organisations have broken out a number of specialist operations, such as computing or training, as profit centres. Such delegation implies a high degree of both responsibility and authority. It may include the hire and fire of labour, the supply of materials, the placing of sub-contracts and even major items of capital expenditure. In an increasing number of cases, profit centres are being given authority to *out-source*; to buy from an external supplier a supply of parts or a service previously provided from within the organisation.

The establishing of profit centres will also involve creating a system for *cross-charging* other parts of the organisation for services given and received. This will result in extra paperwork for managers and accountants, but the time and effort involved is usually justified by tighter control.

149

BUDGETARY CONTROL

Probably the commonest and most effective weapon of financial control is a system of budgetary control. A budget is a carefully calculated forecast covering expenditure, income or both for a set future period. It may be broken down by departments, products, branches or in whatever way is helpful. As time elapses, actual figures will be matched against budget. Major discrepancies will require explanation, and un-budgeted expenditure will normally not be allowed.

The setting of budgets and their use for monitoring can be time-consuming – even painful – but has many advantages. It focuses managers' thinking on the financial implications of what they do. It introduces tight disciplines. It makes good planning essential.

For success, managers must be involved in the setting of the budget. It is possible to impose budgets from a high level, but this usually results in a lack of commitment. Variances will then be seen as the fault of those who set impossible targets.

Guidelines will be produced by top management from its strategic plan for the next period of time – usually the financial year. These will state assumptions about the rate of general inflation, likely wage settlements and any other external influences, and indicate relevant policy con-siderations such as plans for expansion or the need for belt-tightening.

The forecasts will be detailed using the same headings as the financial accounts; income and expenditure codes are frequently used. The budget will also be broken down by suitable periods; weeks, months or accounting periods. Each manager's proposal will normally be reviewed at a higher level within the organisation and the projections amalgamated to produce a corporate budget.

As the financial year progresses, results will be collected, analysed under the budget headings, and the figures for their own operation communicated to individual managers. Adverse variances – higher costs or lower income – will naturally call for action. Many managers, particularly in the public sector, also feel the need to meet their expenditure targets, on the grounds that if they do not, these will be reduced in subsequent years. This sometimes leads to the worst fault of budgetary control – uncontrolled spending as the end of the financial year approaches.

150

Fig. 10.4 Budget

XYZ LTD
TRAINING DEPARTMENT
BUDGET, 1992–3

Code	Activity	This period			Year to date		
		Budget	Act	Var	Budget	Act	Var
	Income	£	£	£	£	£	£
01	Sale of places	1,000	800	(200)	5,000	3,500	(1,500)
02	Sale of material	2,000	0	(2,000)	4,000	5,000	+1,000
	Total	3,000	800	(2,200)	9,000	8,500	(500)
	Expenditure						
11	Staff costs	4,000	4,000	0	10,000	9,500	+500
12	Consumables	1,000	250	+750	3,000	2,000	+1,000
13	Travel & Subsist	2,500	3,000	(500)	7,500	8,500	(1,000)
	Total	7,500	7,250	+250	20,500	20,000	+500
	Total contribution	(4,500)	(6,450)	(1,950)	(10,500)	(11,500)	

Occasionally, it may be felt desirable to produce a budget from a completely blank sheet of paper – *zero-based budgeting*. This technique offers the opportunity to challenge not only the current figures, but the activities they represent; 'Do we need to go on doing this?' 'Does it need to be done in this way?'

► **Checkpoint 10.3**

Does your organisation have a management accountant? If not, how do you keep a check on the financial viability of your operation? Does your operation have cost or profit centres, and if so, are they an advantage? Do you have a budgetary responsibility, and if so, is it a help in managing?

COSTS AND COSTING

Cost accountancy is a major element of management accounting. Its aim, as the name implies, is to provide managers with the best data possible about the costs of what they do and produce or might do or produce. Traditionally, cost accountants have been employed to cost physical process and products but the approach is valid in any area.

Costs are frequently split into *variable costs*, which are incurred as an immediate result of doing something (making a product) and *fixed costs*, which are an appropriate share of all other costs of the organisation (rates, management salaries, building repairs and maintenance). The split between the two is similar to the split between the items included in the trading account (variable costs) and the overhead items in the profit and loss account (fixed costs). However, costing will normally be undertaken not for the whole organisation, or even a major part of it, but for a specific product, product line, service or activity. In doing this, cost accountants enable managers to answer the questions: 'Does what I am doing (or what I am proposing to do) pay?' and 'What if I did it differently?'

Costing is not as easy at it may sound, as all honest motorists know. What is the 'cost' of my journey? Is it sufficient to consider only the additional movement costs (petrol, extra wear-and-tear) – the variable costs? As with our private motoring, there is always a temptation for managers to justify this approach, pointing out that the fixed costs (insurance, depreciation, tax etc.) will continue whether a particular piece of business (or the journey) is undertaken or not. But honest motorists know that their fixed costs must be taken into account somewhere, and honest managers know that the same applies to their fixed costs.

There may, occasionally, be justification for selling at a price that covers only *marginal costs* – the additional cost of making an extra item, or undertaking an extra service. This may be justified to keep machinery

151

occupied or employees working for short periods and in special circumstances, but only when there is strong probability that normal conditions (allowing the recovery of total costs) will return quickly. The more we sell on a marginal cost basis, the higher must be the price of everything else if we are not to go out of business.

Discounted cash flow is a technique for calculating the true cost of a project or activity. It takes account of the financial cost of spending money at a given point in time; the lost interest (or interest paid, if the money is borrowed) and the likely fall in the value of money over the period in question because of inflation.

Capital equipment is frequently costed on the basis of purchase price only. However, this does not take into account the costs of maintenance and repair, consumables and finance. A more useful approach is *life-cycle costing*, in which all these costs are taken fully into account and spread, as accurately as possible, over the expected life of the equipment.

► Checkpoint 10.4

Do you have a cost accountant within your organisation, and if so, do you have contact with them? If not, how do you cost the elements of your operation?

11

The customer

> - **External and internal customers**
> - **The elements of customer service**
> - **The pre-ordering climate**
> - **Placing an order**
> - **From order to delivery**
> - **Packaging/presentation**

We have been a long time getting to the reason for every manager's existence, but at last, we have arrived. Theodore Levitt says:

> **The purpose of a business is to get and keep a customer.**

The customer is the centre of all that we do.

External and internal customers

Every manager has customers – either inside or outside the organisation. Many have direct contact with external customers – the customers of the organisation. For some, such as those in the sales function, external customers are at the centre of their job. Other managers – in production, for example – have only occasional contact with external customers. But all must have their internal customers – those within their organisation to whom they provide a service.

In a typical organisation, departments can be divided into two types. The 'core' activities – R & D, production, marketing and sales – each have a specific service relationship with one or two other departments. The 'service' departments – personnel, finance, and computing – serve all others.

Supplying department	Customer department(s)
R & D marketing, production	marketing, production
marketing	sales
production	sales
personnel/human resources	all
finance/accountancy	all
computer/IT	all

▶ **Checkpoint 11.1**
Who are your (a) external and (b) internal customers? Who, within your organisation, serves you?

154 The elements of customer service

Customer service is sometimes known as 'customer care', a term which emphasises the inter-personal relationship aspect of service. This aspect is important, but 'being nice to the customer' is only one part of customer service. Customer service is a much more far-reaching activity, and may be defined as:

> **CUSTOMER SERVICE**
> **Secondary activities undertaken by an organisation to maximise customer satisfaction in its primary activities.**

The primary activities of a car manufacturer, for example, are to design, make and sell cars. Its secondary, customer service, activities will include the production of owners' maintenance manuals, providing a continuing supply of spare parts, and handling customer complaints. The primary activities of a restaurant are to cook and sell meals to diners. Its secondary, customer service, activities include the supply of menus, table service, and the decor of the dining room. The primary activities of a bus company are the operation of buses on which passengers pay to travel. Its secondary, customer service, activities should include the production and posting of timetables, information about delays and cancellations, and the provision of clean vehicles.

Customer service includes a number of elements, which follow the sequence of a business transaction. These may be called the *customer service sequence*.

THE CUSTOMER SERVICE SEQUENCE

- The pre-ordering climate
- Placing an order
- From order to delivery
- Packaging/presentation
- Delivery
- Handling complaints
- Payment
- After-sales service and support

The application of the sequence to external customer service is obvious. As an example of internal service, we may consider the service provided by the human resources function in helping to fill a vacancy in another department.

INTERNAL CUSTOMER SERVICE – FILLING A VACANCY

■ Pre-ordering climate	The reputation of the department
■ Placing an order	Notifying a vacancy
■ From order to delivery	Waiting for applications
■ Packaging/presentation	The way applications are presented for the manager's consideration
■ Delivery	All aspects of the shortlisting, interview and notification arrangements
■ Handling complaints	Sorting out the manager's feedback on hitches
■ Payment	Inter-departmental cross-charge arrangements
■ After-sales service and support	Help in induction of the new starter and overcoming any initial problems

---

F

▶ **Checkpoint 11.2**

Apply each element of the customer service sequence to your own work, either with internal or external customers.

The pre-ordering climate

The pre-ordering climate includes the knowledge and image of our operation among customers and potential customers. The first question must always be: 'Do they know of our existence?' We are so taken up by the reality of our own existence, that the possibility that someone has not heard of us may not seem credible. But many operations get no further; potential customers do not know they are there. Sadly, this often proves to be the case – even *within* an organisation.

The next question must be: '*what* do they know of us?' The same thinking applies here; *we* know all there is to know about us, but others may know little, and what they think they know may be mistaken. We shall have fewer customers if they think we only sell to the trade, when we are striving to sell to the widest retail market; that our goods are for the use of senior citizens when we aim to appeal to teenagers; that they are only for professionals when we want to be used by all.

Next comes: *how* do they find out about us? Are we in all the relevant directories? Are there easy sources of reference for those wishing to learn about our business, such as magazines or handbooks? Is our sales literature suitable for first-time buyers, or only for experts? Do we have a trade or professional association that helps to create our image? Do we have regular contacts with the media? Are our telephonists and receptionists well-trained and helpful? Their role is often critical during this phase.

▶ **Checkpoint 11.3**

If you had never heard about your organisation and its field of activity, how might you find out (a) by chance, (b) if you felt it important to know? Do you feel your answers to these questions are satisfactory? If not, what should be done?

Placing an order

Having decided that they want to order, customers do not always find the actual process easy or friendly. Many organisations have procedures which are designed to help them rather than their customers. Many, especially in the public sector (plus banks, building societies and insurers) expect customers to complete lengthy and difficult forms that ask for unnecessary or repetitive information. Computerisation has led to a proliferation of numbers; customers may be asked to quote several lengthy sequences of digits to make one order.

Customers who are partly sighted or partly literate often have problems in ordering, even when they are within our target market.

The medium by which orders are placed may be restricted by convention or the convenience of the organisation. Some may insist on personal attendance; others may refuse to accept telephone or fax orders; others require completion of particular paperwork. Only a few accept computer-to-computer orders, despite the advances in information technology. If face-to-face ordering is expected, the customer may feel that the presence of a salesperson is intrusive and pressurising. Some ordering procedures, on the other hand, may offer no help to the puzzled or uncertain.

157

New or inexpert customers (in the building or computer supply industries, for example) may have problems with terminology, or even in knowing what they need. There may be odd custom or practice relating to quantities; things may be sold by reams, quires, the gross, the box or punnet. They may be sold by weight, number, value, or only in odd combinations. The difference between a day return ticket, an away-day, a saver, a supersaver and a 'standard' return ticket, for example, may be incomprehensible to the customer.

The 'small print' of order forms is a frequent source of annoyance. There is legislation about forms of contract, but the customer service angle is still neglected. Customers of monopoly suppliers (whether public or private) often feel they are ordering under duress.

► **Checkpoint 11.4**

Who do our customers (internal or external) contact when they wish to order, and how are they expected to do it? Is there paperwork to be completed? Is it straightforward for them? Are there problems with terminology or order quantities? If they have problems, how do we help our customers?

From order to delivery

This is the period that customers fear most. They have been promised delivery by a certain time or date, but will the promise be met? The worry is the same whether goods or services are to be delivered. The awaited arrival of a bus, train or doctor's appointment causes the same anxieties as the wait for urgently-needed spare parts.

The situation is the same whether the customer is internal or external. Indeed, some of the worst customer service occurs between colleagues within the same organisation; the late set of data, the unanswered memo, the telephone message delivered days afterwards.

We do no favours to ourselves or our customers by making promises we cannot keep. Almost any customer will prefer the promise of a slower delivery which is kept, than of a faster delivery that is not kept. The inconvenience and expense of failed delivery promises can be great. Customers can make fruitless trips into town or keep plant and labour waiting.

Even worse than delayed delivery is lack of information on the expected length and reason for a delay. Passengers wait helpless at bus-stops, motorists sit in the reception area of a garage, house-buyers look despairingly in each day's mail for the draft contract. In the out-patients' department of many hospitals, waiting patients who dare to enquire may even be subject to abuse for their pains.

The answer to such problems can only be proper discipline, from the responsible manager downwards. Managers who are unaware of such problems, or of their customers' difficulties, are failing in a key area.

► **Checkpoint 11.5**

Have you suffered from unkept delivery promises in your working or private life? What did you do about it? Have you failed to keep promises of delivery? Why? What did your customers do about it, and what action did you take?

Packaging/presentation

Packaging is not part of the goods, but an essential part of customer service. This also is true of both goods and service: the way a meal is presented is as important as the quality of the cooking; the typing, layout and presentation of the report has as much impact as its content; our dress and turnout at a meeting will impress the others present as strongly as anything we say.

▶ **Checkpoint 11.6**

What is the equivalent of 'packaging' for the internal service for which you are responsible? Does this packaging create a favourable impression on your customers? If not, how can you improve it? Is the packaging of your external goods or services satisfactory?

159

DELIVERY

No-one feels well-disposed to an organisation that dumps a heap of sand at the entrance to their drive, refuses to help with manoeuvring a heavy case, bangs a plate of food on the table in front of them, or gives them information in a curt, unfriendly way. The act of delivery is an important aspect of customer service.

Interpersonal skills and effective communication can be crucial in this phase. If our service (the provision of information, for example) is given over a counter, it must be given politely, helpfully, with a smile and an appropriate response to individual customers and their needs.

If our service is given over the telephone, whoever gives it must be skilled in telephone technique. Many a customer has given up using a service not because of the quality or accuracy of what they were told over the telephone, but because of the tone of voice or manner of speech of the person telling them. No-one, whether external customer or colleague, enjoys being barked at, spoken to in a couldn't-care-less manner, being kept waiting without explanation (whether before or after connection), being disconnected or transferred to a wrong extension, having their message not delivered or delivered wrongly, or being passed from one extension to another round an organisation. Every manager must understand the dangers of such behaviour, and ensure that no-one in their operation, least of all themselves, is guilty of it. Telephone training is readily available, and can be worth its weight in gold in retaining customer goodwill.

> ▶ **Checkpoint 11.7**
> *Have you suffered from poor delivery of goods or services by colleagues within your own organisation? If so, what went wrong, why, and what should have been done to correct matters? Are you aware of problems suffered by your internal or external customers over the service you provide, and if so, what are they and what are you doing about it? Have you or your staff been trained in telephone use?*

COMPLAINTS HANDLING

To receive a complaint worries most people, but, provided we do not get too many of them, they can be an invaluable aid to good customer service. Complaints are spontaneous feedback from the customer; something that can be difficult and expensive to get in other ways. Often, they provide an opportunity to win over a customer, and make them a friend for life. By viewing complaints positively, we gain an opportunity to improve our customer service for the future.

To gain the advantages, three things are necessary; the correct attitude, good procedures and proper records.

The correct attitude

Most people are naturally defensive – possibly guilty – in their reaction to complaints. In consequence, they may contribute to the dissatisfaction of the complainant, and are less likely to listen effectively and act positively. Training in handling complaints can help, and managers must lead, firstly by example, and secondly by appropriate support for their staff.

When complaints are made face-to-face, it helps to:

- Listen actively
- Give the complainant 'air-time'; the opportunity to express their feelings fully
- If necessary, help the complainant to express themselves
- Do not respond aggressively
- Establish the facts; ask questions when necessary
- Form a cool assessment

- Tell the customer what action you will take
- Keep any promises you have made
- Respond as soon as possible

Procedures

The procedures for handling complaints should be clear and known by all who might be involved. The responsibility for deciding on the response must depend on the seriousness of the complaint. Authority for handling them should be devolved as far down the line as possible.

Record-keeping

To get maximum benefit from complaints, they should be recorded, the records analysed at intervals, and the findings passed to all parts of the organisation that are involved.

161

▶ **Checkpoint 11.8**
Have you complained recently, either to a colleague or an external supplier? If so, how effectively was your complaint handled? Have you or your department received complaints recently? If so, are you satisfied with the way they were handled, recorded and with the use subsequently made of the information?

PAYMENT

Payment can often cause problems with customers – even internal customers, if a system of cost or profit centres and associated cross-charging is operated.

The need is to obtain prompt and full payment without alienating or offending. Managers or other staff who have been in contact with customers during the earlier phases of a transaction are usually the people who should start this process. If there are problems, we may later have to call for help from financial and, possibly, legal specialists.

▶ **Checkpoint 11.9**
Do you have any internal or external problems with payment? If so, how have you handled them, and with what success?

AFTER-SALES SERVICE AND SUPPORT

Buying should be the start of a relationship, not the end. Customers who have bought frequently need further help. They may not know how to properly install or use what they have bought, or how to get the best from its features. If they do not, they will blame our product. They should know that the supplier will respond helpfully to any problems; even those of their own making. Customers who cannot get what they want from us will go elsewhere next time.

This will often mean the provision of operating or installation instructions – even manuals; some suppliers regard these as frilly add-ons, but they can be crucial to customer satisfaction. It may mean guidance, face-to-face, or by means of a telephone help-line. In some cases, it may even call for customer training, either as part of the package, or as a purchased extra.

162

Repairs and spare parts should be readily available. The policy of cutting off the supply or charging excessively for spares may be counter-productive in the long run.

Occasional enquiries, surveys and follow-up of past customers can be a very useful marketing tool, provided such enquiries are not too insistent or intrusive.

▶ **Checkpoint 11.10**
What after-sales service and support does your organisation offer to external customers? Is it satisfactory, and if not, how should it be improved? Do you give or receive any kind of internal 'after-sales service'? If so, is this satisfactory?

12

The context of management

■ **The organisational context**
■ **The organisational drive profile**
■ **Organisational culture**
■ **Managerial style**
■ **The market context**
■ **The external context**

Management cannot be carried out in a vacuum. Managers must always consider the effects of what they do (and do not do) on the world outside their own bailiwick, and they must be aware of that world's effects on them.

This 'world outside' the individual manager has three widening and concentric circles:

- The organisational context
- The market context
- The external context

The organisational context

No manager is an island. In the public or private sector, we must work in the context created by the owners of our organisation and our fellow managers. Unless the owner is a sole trader, the owners will be represented by a policy-making body; a board, council or whatever, possibly supported by a number of committees. Mangers who do not understand or correctly interpret the wishes of this body will have problems.

We can consider the organisational context from two angles: the organisation's *main drive* and its *culture*.

The organisational drive profile

Every organisation has its driving forces, which underlie everything it does. The main organisational drives are:

- The product
- Profit
- The employee
- The customer
- Charity
- Ethics or religion

No organisation will have a single drive, but most will have one which is much stronger than the others. The mix may change. A takeover or other change in ownership often can bring about a radical shift. A new chief executive may alter the balance overnight. A well-managed organisation will respond to changes in the marketplace.

PRODUCT-DRIVEN ORGANISATIONS

Product-driven organisations find the main-spring of their activities in their product, in which owners, managers and employees take immense pride and personal interest. The strength of the organisation has often come from the success of one product (or service). It may have grown from the specialist skill of one individual, and that person may remain in charge as chairman, chief executive or both. The board may contain a large number of people who are experts in a specific field; mechanical engineers, for example, or educationalists.

Many precision engineering businesses are product-driven. Railway companies have traditionally been strongly product-driven. In the public sector, both education and medical sectors have been product-driven.

Product-driven organisations create a clear corporate identity which is a powerful marketing asset. But they will place their own idea of perfection above the need of the customer. They will be reluctant to change the product to meet changes in the marketplace. They will be more concerned about the characteristics of their product than about its profitability or, in the public sector, its cost.

PROFIT-DRIVEN ORGANISATIONS

Profit-driven organisations are those in which the main yardstick for success is profit – the 'bottom line'. Typically organisations in the financial sector, holding companies and marketing organisations tend to be profit-driven. Such organisations are likely to be led by individuals who have the reputation of dynamic entrepreneurs – even 'get rich quick' types. Their board will probably include a fair number of accountants. By definition, the profit drive is exclusive to the private sector.

Profit-driven organisations are often large, and many operate from a multinational base. They may have no clear public image, if only because their trading may be done under a changing variety of names and trademarks. They may survive when others are going to the wall. They will buy or sell subsidiaries and engage in take-over battles. They will be prepared to diversify or shut down operations without hesitation, and will move into and out of markets and product ranges. They may shift their operations from one country to another, according to tax and other cost advantages. If financial considerations dictate, they will be ruthless in making employees redundant.

165

EMPLOYEE-DRIVEN OPERATIONS

Employee-driven operations will tend, if only subconsciously, to regard the provision of employment as a principle reason for their existence. This approach appears to be an ingredient within some public sector organisations. It is also an ingredient in a few private sector companies with paternalistic policies – typically long-established family firms and those which have a strong base within a community, possibly as the only large employer.

Employee-driven organisations often have powerful trade union involvement. They may pay little attention to the needs of customers, and can even come to regard them as a nuisance. Many suffer from lax financial discipline, and carry on board large numbers of supernumerary personnel.

CUSTOMER-DRIVEN ORGANISATIONS

Customer-driven organisations are characterised by willingness to listen to and understand the needs of customers and potential customers. They are flexible in their approach, unbureaucratic, and often have a decentralised structure. Some national retailing and hospitality groups have led the way in this approach, which is becoming common in all sectors.

Of all organisational drives, the customer drive has fewest inherent faults, and many now see this as a model to follow.

CHARITABLE, ETHICAL AND RELIGIOUS ORGANISATIONS

The drive in such organisations is usually explicit, and clearly understood among employees and customers. There are, however, one or two organisations in which the ethical or religious beliefs of the owners or senior executives have been grafted on to other drives and activities. This may spring a trap for an unwary or uninformed manager.

166

Organisations in this category may experience greater internal political pressures than others. The personal commitment of individuals to an ideal may be regarded as more important than their job competence.

▶ **Checkpoint 12.1**

Consider the drive profile of your own organisation by ranking the importance it attaches to each of the drives. Do the same, from your knowledge, for a hospital, a major multinational company, a public monopoly and a charity. Compare the profiles you have produced with those produced by friends or colleagues. Is the drive profile for your organisation appropriate, or would you like to see it altered? If so, how?

ORGANISATIONAL CULTURE

Organisational drive and the style of individual managers converge in terms of organisational culture. This defines what is regarded as acceptable and unacceptable behaviour – 'the way we do things here'. It is seen most clearly in organisations such as the army and some educational institutions, where it may become fossilised as tradition and ceremony. However, it exists in every organisation.

Individual managers must understand the organisational culture. If we do not conform, we run risks. This does not mean that conformity is mandatory; we may choose to go our own way for reasons of efficiency or just personal choice. But we must be aware of what we are doing and the risks involved. The chance of any one individual breaking the mould will be slight, unless they are either in charge or endowed with exceptional strength of purpose and character.

To some extent, management culture is determined by the *overall norms of society*. The management culture that would be expected and accepted from a mid-Victorian mill-owner would probably lead to an immediate walk-out today; the culture expected of Chinese managers almost certainly would be unacceptable in the United States. Attempts to graft Japanese management culture on to western organisations have met with mixed success.

Culture is affected by the *nature and purpose*, or *mission* of the organisation. The management culture within a prison, a slave-galley, a university, a television production unit, an engineering company may be expected to differ (despite contrary evidence from disaffected inmates).

167

Specific situations will also affect management culture, at least temporally. The culture within an army in battle will differ from that of the same army in a time of peace. The culture adopted by an organisation facing a major financial crisis will be different from its culture in times of stability and expansion.

Attitude to change is a key element in organisational culture. The speed of change has accelerated remorselessly in almost every area since the industrial revolution. Before this time, the most dramatic changes were the result of wars and political upheaval; other changes were few and slow. In the last years of the 20th century, managers are faced with continuing change on every front; social, economic, technological. The way organisations and their managers face – even lead – change has become crucial.

The *style* in which individual managers approach their task will be a major element of the organisational culture. While some managers are more inclined to conform to the general norm, others will tend to an individual, even idiosyncratic approach. The latter will naturally contribute more to the culture of their organisation (for better or worse) unless they adopt a style so different that they are rejected by their colleagues. There are two classic approaches to the analysis of managerial style; the *managerial grid* and *situational management*.

Managerial style

Blake and Mouton, in their Managerial Grid,[1] analyse style in terms of the degree to which managers are concerned about the task to be achieved and the people whom they control. From this they identify four basic styles: low task/low people ('uninvolved'); low task/high people ('country club'); high task/low people ('slave-driver') and high task/high people ('involved'). The implication is that the style of the effective manager will be 'involved' – high on both the task and people dimensions.

From a similar starting point, Hersey and Blanchard[2] emphasise that an effective style will vary according to the situation; their approach is known as situational management. For them, the appropriate degree of involvement in both people and task depends on the maturity and effectiveness of the team and the nature of the situation confronting it. Even the *uninvolved* style (low on task and people dimensions) will be appropriate with a highly experienced and successful team that the manager knows well.

► **Checkpoint 12.2**
   What style do you feel is appropriate for your own manager in his present circumstances? How closely do you feel his actual approach matches this?

The market context

The market context of management is made up of all those organisations or individuals with which we have, or might have, business transactions, and those with which we are in competition. These will include:

- Customers and potential customers
- Suppliers and potential suppliers
- Potential employees
- Trade unions
- Competitors

It is in this context, more than any other, that businesses and their

---

[1] Robert R. Blake and Jane S. Mouton, *The Managerial Grid*, Gulf, 1964.
[2] Paul Hersey and Ken Blanchard, *Management of Organisational Behaviour*, Prentice Hall, 1988.

managers succeed or fail. It was pointed out in Chapter 11 that each department within an organisation has its own, internal, customers. For this reason, the 'market context' is partly external and partly internal.

If we have customers, marketing will be part of our role. The Chartered Institute of Marketing defines marketing as:

MARKETING
The management process responsible for identifying, anticipating and satisfying customer requirements profitably.

There is sometimes confusion between marketing and selling. Selling is:

SELLING
The obtaining of orders for goods or services.

Levitt[1] summarises the position: 'selling focuses on the needs of the seller: marketing on the needs of the buyer.' More than anything, both marketing and selling are an attitude of mind. The world does not owe us a living – we must carve one out for ourself. As the motto says: 'If we don't sell, something dreadful happens – nothing.'

▶ **Checkpoint 12.3**
Which elements of the market context affect you most directly? How well-informed are you about the current state of the others? Do you or your department actively market or sell your services (internally or externally)?

The external context

The external context of management is the outermost of the three circles, and its boundaries are infinite. Its elements include:

- Technology
- Geography
- Politics and the law
- International affairs

- Economics
- Social pressures
- Environmental issues

Each of these is now considered.

[1] Theodore Levitt, *The Marketing Imagination*, New York Free Press, 1983.

TECHNOLOGY

Managers can only work within the bounds of the technology available to them. The speed of technological change continues to accelerate in almost every area. Making full use of available technology now requires the sensitivity to recognise and the willingness to embrace on-going change.

Change must be both personal and organisational. Personally, managers must update their own skills and knowledge; their development must be continuous. Organisationally, we must lead the process of adaptation, ensuring that products, services and processes make the best of current technology. This adaptation can be painful, requiring retraining, relocation or even redundancy.

Technological change affects the skills needed by both workforce and manager. Today, we need to be skilled in selecting, developing and training, motivating and controlling people who harbour knowledge and intellectual skills that would have been useless in workers 50 years ago.

It is essential that we know currently available technology that might affect our operation, and what is being used by our colleagues and competitors. We must also be creative and imaginative, examining possible new uses for whatever is on offer. We may even need to stimulate appropriate research and development.

170

▶ **Checkpoint 12.4**

How has your organisation been affected by technological changes in recent years? Have such changes affected the product or service, the methods of working, or both? How have they affected you and how did you respond to the situation?

THE GEOGRAPHICAL CONTEXT

The location of our operation, both the immediate site and the surrounding area, will affect the way in which we manage.

The provision of good national and local infrastructure – rail, road, water and air transport facilities; utilities such as water, electricity and gas; services such as rubbish disposal, street lighting and housing – are matters of general public interest. Some organisations will contribute to them by, for example, providing a private rail siding, an access road or even company housing.

We may have little direct involvement with such questions, but they, or problems associated with them, will affect the way we manage and the success of our efforts. In such areas, we might exercise pressure on public authorities – local councils or central government – or possibly work with other organisations for mutual benefit.

The regional problems that have for long plagued some areas have also been the subject of much government attention and a range of financial incentives. There are currently various grants available that can be very significant when considering re-location or starting up new operations.

▶ **Checkpoint 12.5**

Do any aspects of infrastructure or location affect your operation? If so, what and how? Is there any way you can control, benefit from or mitigate these effects?

171

THE POLITICS AND THE LAW

There is little a manager can now do that is not affected by the law. The laws of the European Community, the United Kingdom, the by-laws of a local authority or even international law: all may influence us.

Law embodies the beliefs of government, and thus reflects the fluctuations of political power. The first act of almost every incoming government is to change aspects of the law affecting managers. Most managers regret this, and feel it makes their work much harder. Indeed, what managers have called for more than anything else has been stability; confidence that their plans will not be destroyed overnight by the stroke of a politician's pen. It is possible to play the game by all sorts of different rules, but it is quite impossible to play if the rules are changed every few minutes. Sadly, politicians have not, so far, got this message.

Because of this, many managers make their views on proposed legislation known before it is too late, either by individual approaches to government, through their members of Parliament, or through their trade or professional organisation. The process of law-making within the UK usually includes the publication of White Papers or other consultative documents, on which all are entitled to comment. Whilst the chance of our view affecting the ultimate outcome will be slight, it is always worth trying, and those who make no comments have less right to complain afterwards.

Groups dedicated to changing aspects of society have proliferated and become more sophisticated and powerful recently. Apart from seeking to pressurise legislators, they often work directly on managers and their organisations. There is no limit to the interests of such groups, but amongst the most active in recent years have been groups concerned with:

- Women's interests
- Road building and traffic (for and against)
- Sunday observance
- Wildlife and animal rights
- Pollution

We will need to be alert to possible involvement with such concerns, and move with great care and sensitivity in handling them.

In recent years there has been much legislation which can affect the way managers go about their work.

AREAS IN WHICH THE LAW AFFECTS MANAGEMENT

- Ownership (nationalisation/privatisation)
- Taxation
- Health and safety at work
- Discrimination (religious, racial and sexual)
- Training and education
- Land-use planning
- Trade unions and industrial relations
- Contracts of employment
- Company law
- Patents, copyright and intellectual property
- Regional support

We must not attempt to be our own lawyers; in law, perhaps more than in any other area, a little knowledge can be a dangerous thing. Modern legislation is so voluminous and complex that the legal profession itself is splintering and specialising in ever smaller areas. But we do need, like other citizens, to know the most important provisions of those aspects of the law most likely to concern us. Health and safety at work and racial and sexual discrimination are amongst the most important of these aspects for most managers.

European Community legislation is also becoming increasingly important within the UK, and completion of the single European market makes it even more so from 1993 onwards. We need to keep up to date in this area also, and know where to go for reliable advice.

▶ **Checkpoint 12.6**

How has your job been affected by legislation within the last few years? How well do you know the provisions of this legislation? Where would you go for advice?

INTERNATIONAL AFFAIRS

International factors affecting management include:

- Currency devaluations and fluctuations
- Blockades and embargoes
- Tariffs
- Treaty obligations
- Wars

Such factors can be devastating to the organisation that is caught unawares. As managers we must keep our eye on current affairs – especially those aspects which could affect our operation. We are also well-advised to form contingency plans against events which, however unlikely, could have a serious effect on us – devaluation, change of government and so on.

It is also true, that as with other unfortunate events, even international difficulties can offer openings; every crisis is an opportunity for the alert manager.

▶ **Checkpoint 12.7**

Has your work ever been directly affected by international political factors, and if so in what way? Did you or your organisation do anything to minimise this effect? Have you contingency plans for events which might affect you?

ECONOMICS

The economic climate can be fundamental to management success or failure. Its elements include:

- General level of prosperity
- Demand for goods and services in various market sectors
- Cost of borrowing money
- Supply and cost of materials
- Supply and cost of labour

The greatest difficulty in this area is to forecast trends. There is a tendency to assume that a trend will continue for ever; that rising prosperity will go on rising; that falling prices will go on falling. Forecasting in connection with manpower planning, in particular, has proved a minefield. Managers who rely on long apprenticeships or traineeships to fulfil their trained manpower needs have frequently found the balance between supply and demand impossible to maintain.

There is always the temptation to rely on advice from 'experts'. Comparing the range of expert economic opinion at any point in time demonstrates that, sadly, such people can see into the future little, if at all, better than the rest of us. Wise managers will rely as little as possible on broad economic forecasting. All we can do is to remain alert and responsive, work to flexible plans and develop contingencies against those problems we can foresee as possible.

The subject of forecasting was discussed in Chapter 9.

▶ **Checkpoint 12.8**
How has your area been affected by economic trends? Have you been able to forecast, anticipate or respond effectively, or have you suffered from unexpected developments?

THE SOCIAL CONTEXT

There are a number of social aspects that can affect the work of managers. These include:

- Demography
- Culture, customs, ethnic and religious factors
- Fashion
- Language

Demographic factors

The age profile of the population can affect organisations through their use of labour and the market for their products or services.

Demography will have a major impact on the sources of labour, and affect policies on recruitment, training, retention and retirement. The effects of the present shortage of school leavers in the UK, for example, have been masked by the recession, but when this comes to an end, the shortage may well rapidly become crucial.

Age distribution will also affect marketing methods and the product mix through the variations of interest and of disposable income within various age groups. Here also, it may be that within the UK the response of some industries to a steadily-aging population has been slow.

Culture and customs

175

Cultural factors are likely to have most impact on the task of managers seeking to export to unfamiliar areas or working as expatriates or within a culture with which they are not familiar. However, the 'unfamiliar areas' may not necessarily mean another country; distinctions within regions of the UK, for example, may be important, either in working practices (hours of work, holidays) or in terms of the marketplace.

In such circumstances, we will need sound guidance on such cultural differences and how they might affect us. If the culture is very different from the one we know best, we will need to examine its implications before making any important decisions such as whether and how to enter a new market or relocate an operation.

Ethical, religious and cultural beliefs often pass through into political action. Wise managers keep a weather eye on such matters and any possible impact on their work.

Fashion

Changes of fashion have direct effects on those who make and sell clothes and toys. Rather longer-term variations probably affect most industries. Research has suggested the existence of regular cycles in such things, and canny managers will seek evidence in their own areas on which to base forward plans.

LANGUAGE

Language is important to the manager. If we are responsible for any aspect of management involving people whose native language is not our own there will be difficulty. Most managers in this position believe that this problem can only be effectively overcome by becoming proficient in the necessary languages. The rather arrogant attitude of so many native English speakers can only make the manager's task harder, whether as a salesperson or an employer.

▶ **Checkpoint 12.9**
What factors of the social context affect your job situation, and how? Identify one or two of your own leading beliefs (about the 'enterprise culture', 'social responsibility', or 'management ethics') and consider how they affect your approach to the management task. Have you worked as a manager in a culture with which you were not familiar? If so, how did it affect your work?

ENVIRONMENTAL ISSUES

The environmental or 'green' context of management continues to gain in importance, and is now seen by some as fundamental to the future of industrial society. Green concerns cover an immense range of issues; many generate considerable emotion. The unifying thread is the effect of industrial activities on the future quality of life on earth.

It is frequently suggested that industrialisation lies at the heart of these problems, and that the aims of managers and of those who care for the environment must therefore conflict. Whether industrialisation has, in fact, caused more environmental damage than benefit is open to discussion, but it is clearly unjust to blame managers as a group for the environmental deterioration of the past century. This blame must be shared by society as a whole, which has been (and still is) happy to avail itself of the benefits industry has offered.

Unfortunately, the issues are so many and so far-reaching that there is a danger of overlap, blurring and contradiction. The production of biodegradable plastic may, for example, use more energy or the recycling of materials may add to local pollution. Sensible courses of action may be difficult to find. Some industries have already acquired a reputation for exploiting green concern as a sales weapon. In some of the most important green issues, individual managers, unless employed in specific roles, can do no more than private citizens, but there may be others in which we can have an immediate effect. Current green issues include:

- Global pollution
- Local pollution
- Energy conservation
- Conservation of other resources
- General amenity
- Animal welfare

Global pollution

The damage done to the ozone layer, global warming caused by the emission of greenhouse gases, climatic change from the destruction of forests, acid rain, and other world-wide harm from industrial processes or products: these present the clearest long-term challenges to managers. Green activists see such areas as high on the list of those in which managers can set a moral example. Few of us are likely to be in a position to have an immediate effect on such activities, but most will have the opportunity, either in our working or private lives, to exert pressure.

Local pollution

Problems of waste disposal (especially nuclear waste), nuclear radiation and pollution of rivers, soil, beaches and air are to many people the clearest symptoms of uncaring, profit-seeking, socially-irresponsible industry. Many of these problems already are, or are soon likely to be, the subject of legislation. They should be at the forefront of every manager's thinking. As with other legislation, we need to know the current situation as it applies to us, be aware of proposed laws or regulations, make our views on them known, and have contingency plans against changes. Concerned managers will not wait for this to happen but will take any action open to them to eliminate pollution for which they are responsible.

Energy conservation

The massive use of non-renewable energy sources has been one of the clearest factors in the process of industrialisation. First coal and then oil and its derivatives have provided the power to make and move goods worldwide, replacing the water and wind power of earlier times. There may be little we can do about the source of the power we use – setting up a windmill on the company car-park would probably not gain general approval. We can, however, do a good deal to economise on the use of power in heating, lighting, machinery and transport. Fortunately, such economies will also usually translate into higher profits.

Conservation of other resources

Many green activists extend their concerns to the general use of resources, whether non-renewable, such as minerals; renewable (in theory, at least) resources such as timber and other biological products; or finite resources, such as land (and, ultimately, the ocean). The use of material for packaging is a particular target, as are disposable products (kitchen rolls, tissues). Re-cycling of suitable materials (aluminium, glass, paper) is advocated where practicable.

This concern is very far-reaching, and can extend to opposition to the general concept of economic growth. The phrase 'sustainable economy' can be interpreted in more or less restrictive ways, but it probably constitutes the greatest challenge of all to industry and commerce.

Animal welfare

The use of animals for tests and experiments, the conditions in which farm animals are kept, and the effect of industrial processes and pro-ducts of wildlife are highly emotive. Vegetarianism has already become a powerful force within the food and catering industries. Only a limited number of managers are directly affected by such issues, and individuals who are not can only struggle with their own conscience.

General amenity

The image of industry and its 'dark satanic mills' remains powerful. Many green activists are concerned with the development of specific sites, either for general reasons of amenity (including increase in traffic) or because of damage to wild life. Managers who try to ride roughshod over such concerns are likely to run into serious trouble. Sensitivity to such issues, sound advice from experts and consultation with those involved are musts.

The effect of planning legislation within the UK on industry and commerce has varied with the political complexion of local and national governments. In the long term future, green pressures seem likely to make such authorities more restrictive.

The environmental audit

The concept of the environmental audit has grown. It is suggested that managers should examine the direct and indirect environmental impact of their activities at regular intervals, and make any possible adjustments.

179

▶ **Checkpoint 12.10**

What effect does your organisation and its activities have on the environment? Is there anything you can or should do to minimise damage? Do you have personal concerns in this area, and if so, what are their implications for you and other managers? Has your organisation ever carried out an environmental audit?

Bibliography

■

1 What is Management?

Managers Factomatic, 2nd ed, Jack Horn, Englewood Cliffs NJ, Prentice Hall, 1992
Becoming a Manager, Linda A Hill, Boston Mass, Harvard Business School Press, 1992
The Shorter MBA: a Practical Approach to Business Skills, Barrie Pearson and others, London, Thorsons, 1991
Management Theory and Practice, Rob Dixon, Oxford, Made Simple Books, 1991

2 Leadership

The Manager's Short Course, Bill Holton, Cher Holton, New York, John Wiley, 1992
The Superchiefs: the People Principles and Practice of the New Management, Robert Heller, London, Mercury Books, 1992
Frontiers of Leadership: an Essential Reader, Michael Syrett, Clare Hogg eds, Oxford, Blackwell, 1992
Charisma and Leadership in Organisations, Alan Bryman, London, Sage, 1992
Positive Leadership: How to Build a Winning Team, Mike Pegg, London, Mercury Books, 1991
Executive Leadership: a Practical Guide to Managing Complexity, Elliott Jaques, Stephen D Clement, Oxford, Blackwell Business, 1991
Management Teams – Why They Succeed or Fail, Belbin, E Meredith, London, Heinemann, 1981

3 Self Management

Mastering Self Leadership: Empowering Yourself for Personal Excellence, Charles C Manz, Englewood Cliffs NJ, Prentice Hall, 1992
Managing Yourself: Management by Detached Involvement, Jagdish Parikh, Oxford, Basil Blackwell, 1991
Making an Impact in Your New Job: the First 30 Days, Elwood N Chapman, London, Kogan Page, 1990
Self Development in Organizations, Mike Pedler and others, London, McGraw Hill, 1990
Develop Your Management Potential: a Self Help Guide, Charlotte Chambers, John Coopey, Adrian McLean, London, Kogan Page, 1990
Managing Yourself, Mike Pedler, Tom Boydell, Aldershot, Gower in association with Fontana Paperbacks, 1990
Thriving on Chaos: a Handbook for a Management Revolution, Tom Peters, London, Macmillan, 1988

4 Planning

Productive Planning How to Get More Done, James R Sherman, London, Kogan Page, 1991

Making Strategy Happen: Transforming Plans into Reality, Arnold S Judson, Oxford, Basil Blackwell, 1990

Effective Strategic Management: Analysis and Action, Kenneth J Hatten, Mary Louise Hatten, Englewood Cliffs, NJ, Prentice Hall, 1988

Planning Together: the Art of Effective Teamwork, George Gawlinski, Lois Graessle, London, Bedford Square Press, 1988

5 Organisation

Analysing Organisations, 2nd ed, Sandra Dawson, Basingstoke, Macmillan, 1992

Designing Organizations: a Decision Making Perspective, Richard Butler, London, Routledge, 1991

Organizations Structures Processes and Outcomes, 5th ed, Richard H Hall, Englewood Cliffs, Prentice Hall International, 1991

Managing Change, Colin Carnall, London, Routledge, 1991

Parkinson's Law or the Pursuit of Progress, C Northcote Parkinson, Harmondsworth, Penguin Books, 1957

6 Human Resources

Strategies for Human Resource Management: a Total Business Approach, Michael Armstrong ed, Coopers and Lybrand, London, Kogan Page, 1992

Personnel and Profit: the Pay Off from People, Hugo Fair, Institute of Personnel Management, London, 1992

Employee Resourcing, Derek Torrington and others, Institute of Personnel Management, London, IPM, 1991

Personnel Management for the Single European Market, Mark Pinder, London, Pitman, 1990

A Handbook of Human Resource Management, Michael Armstrong, London, Kogan Page, 1990

Managing Human Resources, 2nd ed, Alan Cowling, Chloe Mailer, London, Edward Arnold, 1990

Managing Human Resources, Jane Weightman, Institute of Personnel Management, London, IPM, 1990

7 Managing Operations

Managing Activities and Resources, Roger Bennett, National Extension College, Institute of Supervisory Management, London, Kogan Page, 1989

Handbook of Production and Inventory Control, Nyles V Reinfeld ed, Englewood Cliffs, Prentice Hall, 1987

Effective Problem Solving: a Structured Approach, Dave Francis, London, Routledge, 1990

Health and Safety at Work: Law and Practice, Michael J Goodman, London, Sweet and Maxwell, 1988

Work Measurement, 2nd ed, Dennis A Whitmore, Institute of Management Services, London, Heinemann, 1987

8 Communication

Guide to Managerial Communication, 3rd ed, Mary Munter, Englewood Cliffs NJ, Prentice Hall, 1992

The Handbook of Communication Skills, Bernice Hurst, London, Kogan Page, 1991

Stand and Deliver: a Handbook for Speakers, Chairmen and Committee Members, Rev ed, Kenneth P Brown, London, Thorsons, 1991

You Want me to do What: a Guide to Persuasive Communication, Patrick Forsyth, London, Sheldon Press, 1991

Communicate for Success: How to Manage, Motivate and Lead your People, Eric W Skopec, Reading Ma, Addison Wesley, 1990

Effective Employee Communications, Michael Bland, Peter Jackson, London, Kogan Page, 1990

Communication Problem Solving: the Language of Effective Management, Ian McCall, John Cousins, Chichester, John Wiley, 1990

Improving your Communication Skills, Malcolm Peel, London, Kogan Page, 1990

If only I had said: Conversation Control Skills for Managers, Charles J Margerison, London, Mercury Business Paperbacks, 1990

9 Managing Information

Creative Management, Jane Henry ed, Open University, London, Sage, 1991

Systematic Problem Solving and Decision Making, Sandy Pokras, London, Kogan Page, 1989

Information the Key to Effective Management, Bob Norton, Malcolm Peel, Bradford, MCB University Press, 1989

Effective Meeting Skills, Marion E Haynes, London, Kogan Page, 1988

How to Make Meetings Work, Malcolm Peel, London, Kogan Page, 1988

The New Rational Manager, Charles H Kepner, Benjamin B Tregoe, London, John Martin, 1981

10 Managing Finance

Concise Guide to Company Finance and its Management, R E Brayshaw, London, Chapman and Hall, 1992

Finance in Organisations, Humphrey Shaw, Kings Ripton Huntingdon, Elm Pub, 1991

Understand Business Finance: a Guide for Managers, Ernest Jones, London, Pitman, 1991

Financial Analysis and Control: Financial Awareness for Students and Managers, Alan Birchall, Oxford, Butterworth Heinemann, 1991

Finance for Managers: a Practical Guide for the Non-Financial Manager, Derek Thorn, London, Mercury Books, 1991

How to Master Finance: a No-nonsense Guide to Understanding Business Accounts, Terry Gasking, London, Business Books, 1991

Management of Company Finance, 5th ed, J M Samuels, F M Wilkes, R E Brayshaw, London, Chapman and Hall, 1990

Secrets of Successful Financial Management, D A Hill, L E Rockley, Oxford, Heinemann Professional, 1990

Finance and Accounting for Managers, David Davies, Institute of Personnel Management, London, IPM, 1990

11 The Customer

Customer Service Pocketbook, Tony Newby, Alresford, Management Pocketbooks, 1991

Total Customer Satisfaction: Lessons from 50 Companies with Top Quality Customer Service, Jacques Horovitz, Michele Jurgens Panak, *Financial Times*/Pitman, 1992

Relationship Marketing: Bringing Quality Customer Service and Marketing Together, Martin Christopher, Adrian Payne, David Ballantyne, Oxford, Butterworth Heinemann in association with the Chartered Institute of Marketing, 1991

Customer Service and Support: Implementing Effective Strategies, Colin G Armistead, Graham Clark, London, *Financial Times*/Pitman, 1992

Quality Total Customer Service, Lynda King Taylor, London, Century Business, 1992

Customer Service Planner, Martin Christopher, Oxford, Butterworth Heinemann, 1992

Competitive Customer Care: a Guide to Keeping Customers, Merlin Stone, Laurie Young, Kingston upon Thames, Croner Publications, 1992

Managing Quality Customer Service, William B Martin, London, Kogan Page, 1991

Customer Service: How to Achieve Total Customer Satisfaction, Malcolm Peel, London, Kogan Page, 1987

183

12 The Context of Management

Environmental Auditing: a Guide to Best Practice in the UK and Europe, Lesley Grayson, London, British Library and Technical Communications, 1992

Mission and Business Philosophy: Winning Employee Committment, Andrew Campbell, Kiran Tawadey, Oxford, Heinemann Professional, 1990

Intuition in Organizations: Leading and Managing Productively, Weston H Agor ed, London, Sage, 1989

Peripheralisation and Industrial Change: Impacts on Nations, Regions, Firms and People, G H R Linge ed, London, Croom Helm, 1988

Writers on Organisations, 3rd ed, D S Pugh, D J Hickson, C R Hinings, Harmondsworth, Penguin Books, 1983

Understanding Organizations, 3rd ed, Charles B Handy, Harmondsworth, Penguin Books, 1985

Index

■

184